HAUNTED
PHOENIX

HAUNTED PHOENIX

DEBE BRANNING

Haunted America

Published by Haunted America
A Division of The History Press
Charleston, SC
www.historypress.com

Front cover: author's collection.
Back cover: author's collection; *inset*: courtesy of the Orpheum Theatre.

First published 2019

Manufactured in the United States

ISBN 9781467140928

Library of Congress Control Number: 2019943379

This book is dedicated to the MVD Ghostchasers paranormal team members past, present and future, who have always remained credible and reputable in their paranormal data.

CONTENTS

CONTENTS

ACKNOWLEDGEMENTS

I would like to give a shout-out to all of the knowledgeable paranormal investigative teams, tour guides, tour companies, historians and amazing location owners who willingly shared their information, experiences and tales of the unknown to fill these pages with the phenomena they have encountered. I also want to thank friends and team members who accompanied me while exploring various locations and participating with the interviews.

I often say, "History and mystery go hand in hand," and I am hoping these stories will carry on the legacy of Phoenix for many years to come.

INTRODUCTION

Although Phoenix, Arizona, is recognized as a newer city compared to the metropolises of the eastern United States, it still holds a large amount of paranormal activity within its land and inside the walls of its historic buildings.

The history of the city of Phoenix begins with pioneer Jack Swilling, a Confederate veteran of the Civil War. In 1867, while traveling through the Salt River Valley, he saw a potential for farming, much like the military had already cultivated farther east, near Fort McDowell. He formed a small community that same year about four miles east of the present city. Lord Darrel Duppa, one of the original settlers in Swilling's party, suggested the name *Phoenix*, as it described a city born from the ruins of a former Hohokam civilization that mysteriously vanished into history.

In Rome, the Phoenix was a symbol of the perpetual continuation of the Roman Empire, and the bird was featured on coins as a reminder of the great strength of the empire. Because of its ability to die, rise from the ashes and come back to life again, the meaning of the Phoenix has a foundation of renewal, rebirth and resurrection.

The board of supervisors in Yavapai County, which at the time encompassed Phoenix, officially recognized the new town on May 4, 1868, and the first post office was established the following month, with Swilling as postmaster. On February 12, 1871, the territorial legislature created Maricopa County. The first election for county office was held in 1871, when Tom Barnum was elected Phoenix's first sheriff.

The town grew quickly during the 1870s, and President Ulysses S. Grant issued a land patent for the present site of Phoenix on April 10, 1874. By 1875, Phoenix boasted a telegraph office, sixteen saloons and four dance halls. The early city grid consisted of eight streets running east–west and fifteen streets running north–south. The principle business district was centered on Washington Street just east of Central Avenue.

In the 1880s, the arrival of the railroad in the Salt River Valley was the first of several key events that altered the economy of Phoenix. The city became a trade center, with its products reaching eastern and western markets. By 1881, Phoenix had outgrown its original townsite as people moved in for its ideal climates. In 1888, the city offices were moved into the new Phoenix City Hall at Washington Street and Central Avenue. When the territorial capital was moved from Prescott to Phoenix in 1889, the temporary territorial offices were also located in city hall. With the arrival of the Santa Fe, Prescott and Phoenix Railroad in 1895, Phoenix was connected to Prescott, Flagstaff and other communities in the northern part of the territory. The increased access to commerce expedited the city's economic rise. The year 1895 also saw the establishment of the Phoenix Union High School with an enrollment of ninety students. Beautiful Victorian mansions, the style of the day, began to

1885 bird's-eye view map of Phoenix by C.J. Dyer. *Courtesy of Wikimedia.*

line the prestigious downtown neighborhoods, in contrast to the earlier one-story adobe structures erected with soil and vegetation.

Its canal irrigation system led to a thriving farming community, with many of the original crops, such as alfalfa, cotton, citrus and hay, remaining important parts of the Phoenix economy for decades. Cotton, cattle, citrus, climate and copper were known locally as the "Five Cs" of Phoenix's economy. These pillars of economic success remained the driving forces of the city until after World War II.

On February 14, 1912, Phoenix became the official state capital of Arizona, which was admitted to the Union as the forty-eighth state under President William Howard Taft. Phoenix remains the anchor of the Phoenix Metro area and is also known as the Valley of the Sun.

By 1950, more than 100,000 people lived in Phoenix and the surrounding communities. When the year 2000 rolled around, it had become one of the largest cities in the United States, with 3,000,000 residents. Appropriately, the Phoenix bird was adopted by the city council as its official city symbol in 1987.

With a history of an exploding population growth and land expansion came fast money, greed and competition to get to the top. Sudden accidents, tragedies and murders abounded in the early days of Phoenix. The Wild West was coming to a close, and the modern city was beginning to emerge—like the Phoenix! Some of the early pioneers and restless spirits still remain in the historic buildings, streets and cemeteries, waiting for the opportunity to resurrect once again, much like the celebrated Phoenix.

1
CENTRAL DISTRICT

ST. MARY'S BASILICA

St. Mary's Basilica, officially named the Church of the Immaculate Conception of the Blessed Virgin Mary, is the oldest Catholic parish in Phoenix. In fact, it was the only Catholic parish in Phoenix in 1924. In the beginning, St. Mary's was located at the private residence of Jesus Otero, located at First Avenue and Washington Street. From 1872 to 1881, the priests from Florence, Arizona, traveled by horse and buggy every three months to conduct the Catholic liturgy.

Construction of a church on the present site of Third and Monroe Streets began in 1880 under the supervision of Reverend Edouard Gerard. He was the first priest ordained in Arizona, on February 2, 1877. The simple church was built of adobe with a steeple on a pitched, shingled roof. The church was dedicated by Bishop Salpointe on June 24, 1881.

Soon, the adobe church needed major repairs, and the congregation longed for a larger facility. Miraculously, the pastor received permission from his superiors to begin construction of a new church. This new place of worship would be built in two phases, due to budget constraints. The old adobe church was demolished, and construction began on the basement, which would serve as what Phoenicians called the "basement church" until the upper church could be completed. The architect was Brother Adrian Wewer, OFM. He was assisted by Brother Leonard Darched, OFM. The local architects were R.A. Gray and George Gallagher. The "basement church" (which now serves as the social hall) was dedicated on February 11, 1903, under the patronage of the Immaculate Heart of the Blessed Virgin Mary by His Excellency Bishop Henri Granjon of Tucson.

The second phase of construction began in July 1913. The contractor was W.J. Rifley. The church is an outstanding example of Mission Revival design. The beautiful interior is in the Romanesque style.

The church's structure supports four domes spanning the length of the basilica. All of the domes are a compound design with the pendentives, following Roman architecture, transferring the weight of the roof to the pillars. The center dome is topped with stained glass. St. Mary's has one of the largest stained-glass collections in the state. The dome over the altar is crowned with a cupola designed to provide light to the altar. The two bell towers are topped with onion-shaped domes. The towers house four bells, which ring daily.

On September 6, 1976, St. Mary's Basilica was named an historic site by the Arizona Historical Society. And, on October 17, 1977, the church was added to the State Inventory of Historic Places of Arizona. St. Mary's was placed in the National Register of Historic Places on November 29, 1978. On September 2, 1985, His Holiness Pope Saint John Paul II solemnly proclaimed the church of the Immaculate Conception of the Blessed Virgin Mary to be a Minor Basilica.

Today, St. Mary's Basilica is surrounded by skyscrapers and gives the appearance of an imposing structure in its urban setting.

A gentleman in Phoenix, Arizona, who had a reputation of being both truthful and level-headed, told a story about an uncanny sight he saw on the night of Friday, August 18, 1893. According to the *Arizona Republican*, he kept quiet about what he saw until several days later, when he met another man who had witnessed the same occurrence the following night. The names of both gentlemen were kept on file at the *Republican* office for the inspection of those nonbelievers who delighted in the destruction of immaterial news.

The man recounted his tale:

> *I was on my way home last Friday night some time, I think, before midnight. I live on — street, near —'s place. I always go up Washington to First Street, cross to Monroe and go up Monroe to Fifth. I was walking slowly along the east side of Monroe not thinking of anything. I was neither to the right nor to the left. When I came directly in front of the Catholic Church, I became uneasily aware of a strange presence, though at that moment, I*

saw nothing. I turned involuntary toward the door of the church and what I saw, I will never forget.

In the archway stood two female figures clad in white; they didn't look shadowy as ghosts are supposed to appear, but there was a strange plainness of an outline—luminous and uncanny. I could see their arms distinctly and their feet seemed to be incased in white slippers. Their hands were also unnaturally visible. It is probably twenty feet from where I stood to the archway and the moon had gone down for some hours. It was neither very dark nor very light. I don't think that a substantial object could have been so clearly seen at that distance.

Strangest and most horrible of all, both of the figures were headless. Badly scared as I was, I remember I thought they resembled those mannequins used in a dressmaker's shop.

It seemed to the gentleman that he stood there for thirty minutes. But then he thought perhaps it was nearly half a minute—for time, you know, passes unnaturally slowly or fast under certain paranormal circumstances. When

Spirits were seen in the shadowy arches of St. Mary's Basilica. *Author's collection.*

17

he collected himself, he was standing in the middle of Fourth Street. He was no coward or a superstitious fool, so he began to reason with himself. He didn't believe he had seen anything but tried to convince himself that either his eyes or imagination had played a trick on him. He was determined to solve the mystery, for, unless he did, he feared he would carry away with him a permanent belief in ghosts.

He went back with some hesitation to the opening that leads from the sidewalk to the church. There the frightful pair stood, even plainer, if possible, in a luminous outline and more "headless" than before. He tried to make up his mind to go up to them, and he did go to within maybe ten or fifteen feet. He thought he remained there two minutes. He remembered that on the Tuesday before, there had been the Feast of the Assumption, so he thought this might be some midnight ceremony and that the actors were persons of flesh and blood. But the fiery outline of the figures, the missing heads and the still and dark church were working against his theory. He went away without turning his face until he got halfway back to Fourth Street. He decided to say nothing about the incident and never did mention it until one Sunday, when he heard that a gentleman named Frank had seen something strange in front of the church the very next night. The two gentlemen met and decided to compare notes.

Frank didn't make as much of an investigation as the first man did, but he swore he saw for an instant—and might have seen longer if he hadn't been in a hurry to leave the neighborhood—two women in white standing in the archway.

The gentleman continued to walk home past the church every night but changed his route to the other side of the street after his terrifying sighting. Much to his relief, he did not see the ghosts again.

St. Mary's Basilica Catholic Church
400 East Fourth Street
Phoenix, AZ 85004

Arizona State Capitol

The Arizona State Capitol building in Phoenix was the final home for Arizona's territorial government and already in place when statehood arrived in 1912. Jeered for having what was nicknamed the "State Capital on Wheels," the capital city was switched from Prescott (1864) to Tucson (1867), back to Prescott (1877) and finally to Phoenix in 1889. Initially, all three branches of the new state government were housed in the same four-story structure.

The building was constructed to help demonstrate that the Arizona Territory was ready for long-awaited statehood. It was designed by James Riely Gordon, whose original plan for the capitol was for it to be much larger. He envisioned the new capitol building to be a replica of the United States Capitol in Washington, D.C. Budget restraints scrapped a grand staircase to the second-floor entryway and two legislative wings, and a much smaller lead-alloy top replaced the planned decorative copper dome.

Construction on the capitol began in 1898, and it was ready to serve state officials in 1901. It was built from materials associated with the Arizona Territory, including massive granite stones and hints of copper. Phoenix's population flourished. In 1918, and again in 1938, expansions were added on the west end of the building. An executive tower was added in 1974. The dome was later replaced with real copper and topped with a weather

The early Arizona State Capitol building was completed in 1901. *Courtesy of Wikimedia.*

vane called *Winged Victory*. The Arizona State Capitol is listed in the National Register of Historic Places. The 1901 portion of the capitol is now maintained by the Arizona Capitol Museum.

For several years, I scanned through old newspapers and researched Arizona history at the State Archives Library while it was still located in the capitol building. An archivist approached me one day and said, "You know, there is an interesting energy in the old State Capitol Building. Look it up sometime."

And, indeed I did. Tuesday, May 7, 1912, was just another busy working day at the state capitol. Workmen were doing maintenance construction on the outside of the building and sprucing up the landscape. There were about 150 people inside the building, and the legislature was in session. Upstairs, in the Arizona legislation chambers, politicians were discussing laws that would shape the new state. Downstairs, next to the ground-floor entrance, the clerks in the surveyor general's office worked quietly in their world of maps and land records.

Just before noon, violence interrupted the peaceful setting downstairs near the east entrance. Frank Coffman barged in, turned to his right and, without saying a word, fired four fatal shots at the chief surveyor general clerk, Granville Malcolm Gillett. Coffman then stepped back to the center of the rotunda and fired the gun once more—shooting himself in the heart.

The popping sounds from the gun caught everyone off guard. No one could imagine there would be a shooting in such a place. Many thought it was noise from the construction or the explosion of a harmless bomb by a practical joker. These days, we would all be running for cover!

A coroner's jury determined that Coffman was motivated by an insane fixation on a land deal. He was convinced that Gillett had cheated him, and a note was found in Coffman's pocket stating he felt he had been swindled in a real estate transaction and decided to take things to the limit.

His suicide and Gillett's unexpected death would be a logical reason residual energy could linger at the capitol building. It gave me a better understanding why I always felt uneasy walking near the beautiful mosaic design beneath the center of the rotunda.

Wesley Bolin served as the fifteenth governor of the State of Arizona between 1977 and 1978. He died in his office from a fatal heart attack after serving merely five months on the job. The Wesley Memorial Plaza near the state capitol was named in his honor. It has been said that the former governor is buried within the vast number of patriotic memorials spread across the capital grounds. It is more probable that some of his ashes were scattered in the beautiful rose gardens; this is perhaps the reason the blooms of the flowers continue to be absolutely beautiful!

Arizona State Capitol Museum
1700 West Washington Street
Phoenix, AZ 85007

LUKE-GREENWAY AMERICAN LEGION POST 1

American Legion Post 1 has welcomed veterans from all branches of the United States Armed Forces since 1919. On June 18, 1919, Post 1 was officially organized and dedicated to the memory of Frank Luke Jr. It was the first post chartered in the state of Arizona. In 1939, Frank Luke Jr. Post 1 and John C. Greenway Post 50 merged to become Luke-Greenway American Legion Post 1.

American Legion Post 1 was the first post chartered in Arizona. *Author's collection.*

The post is situated in a building that was once the home of charter member William Pickerell. It was constructed on a former ostrich farm along Seventh Avenue and Polk Street in Central Phoenix. Several add-on rooms have been built to increase the size of the facility throughout the years. When one steps through the door, the vintage décor makes one feel transported in time to the 1960s.

John Lay took on the duties of caretaker of the American Legion building. His wife and two children lived on the site for several years. You see, there is a secret basement apartment below the stage. The family would enter their living quarters through a passageway in the former orchestra pit. Lay was a loyal employee and loved his job more than anything in the world. Although John has passed away, the staff and members of the American Legion still feel his presence.

"We often feel he is there keeping watch over things," a dedicated volunteer proclaimed. "We sense him in the building when we open the doors in the morning. Once we ventured down below to the old apartment and found a folder of the history of the post lying on top of some old boxes. None of us would have placed it there. Nobody had ever seen it before—or knew it even existed! It was as though John Lay sensed we needed the information and wanted us to find it."

Another time, a group of transients, seeking warmth from the cold winter weather, set a fire just outside the building walls. The blaze grew, and the flames burned out of control. The fire department arrived to avert potential disaster. The fire captain noted that a window above the fire had not exploded from the heat.

"I am totally surprised the window did not break." The captain stood puzzled, making his post-fire inspection. He pointed out that stacks of bingo papers were stored in the room just on the other side of the wall near the window. If the fire had gained access to that room, the entire building would have gone up in flames. The members of the post believe John Lay was on the job watching over the building that night, protecting the history and heroic items displayed in the small post museum and keeping them safe from harm's way.

Luke-Greenway American Legion Post 1
364 North Seventh Avenue
Phoenix, AZ 85007

YMCA

The first YMCA in Phoenix was opened in 1892 on the ground floor of a two-story building at First and Washington Streets. This facility served Phoenix for almost twenty years. In the early days, the YMCA was designed to help young men who may have, as they say, "lost their way" and needed a clean place to bathe and sleep.

Money was raised in 1906 to build the first permanent facility, but a recession held back the grand opening until 1911. The three-story building was constructed at Second Avenue and Monroe Street and featured a gymnasium, a swimming pool, club rooms and several residence rooms. The building was designed so that the roof could be raised to add additional floors if needed.

Adding the fourth floor turned out to be a good move. In 1942, the YMCA added a serviceman's dormitory to assist military personnel passing through Phoenix during World War II, giving them a safe location to spend the night.

The YMCA building maintains downtown Phoenix's largest civil defense shelter. *Author's collection.*

After World War II, YMCA director John C. Lincoln proposed construction on yet another building with a modern look. The architecture company Lescher and Mahoney designed the new facility. It reflected the fears of the Cold War and featured downtown Phoenix's largest civil defense shelter. The new Downtown YMCA opened in January 1952.

In 2006, major renovations were completed, along with an addition that offered another seventy-five thousand square feet. The new site for the YMCA was on the west side of First Avenue between Van Buren and Filmore Streets.

Tragedy struck the Phoenix YMCA on December 17, 1946, when Quanah F. Parker, a radio ad salesman for KPHO, was found dead in his room. The police homicide detective stated that Parker, thirty-nine, had slashed his throat, severing the jugular vein and nearly decapitating him.

Joe Atredies, director of Phoenix Ghost Tours, spoke to staff at the YMCA. One ghost story has been told over and over again. It seems that employees and visitors to the Y often see an apparition of a headless specter in the hallways. Although Parker passed away in the YMCA at the earlier location, could he have "lost his way" and is still needing a clean place to lie down in eternal sleep?

Young man, I was once in your shoes
I said, I was down and out with the blues
I felt no man cared if I were alive
I felt the whole world was so tight

That's when someone came up to me
And said, young man, take a walk up the street
There's a place there called the YMCA
They can start you back on your way

YMCA you'll find it at the YMCA

"YMCA," written by Victor Willis, Jacques Moranli, Henri Belolo of the Village People

YMCA
350 First Avenue
Phoenix, AZ 85003

Pueblo Grande Ruins

The Pueblo Grande Museum is located just minutes from downtown Phoenix on a 1,500-year-old archaeological site left by the Hohokam culture, which once thrived in Arizona. The National Historic Landmark is the largest preserved archaeological site within the Phoenix city limits.

The prehistoric Hohokam culture created the archaeological structures and items found at Pueblo Grande. It is believed that this area was settled around AD 450. Due to major population movements, among other factors, the site was abandoned by AD 1450 and literally became a ghost town. It is a mystery as to what became of the Hohokam people. It seems as though they suddenly vanished from the face of the earth.

Pueblo Grande features a large platform mound with retaining walls that were formerly composed of taller walled dwellings. This massive structure contains over twenty thousand cubic meters (yards) of fill. There were also many adobes and at least three ball courts where members from neighboring villages came to trade and compete in early ceremonial games. Construction of the ball courts began by AD 750.

The Hohokam tribe was the first people to practice irrigated agriculture in the area. There are remnants of their irrigation canals at the historic site.

The Pima Indians, who now live in the area, have stated that Pueblo Grande was once the home of Huamanui ("Yellow Buzzard"), the name of a powerful chief.

At sunrise on the summer solstice and at sunset on the winter solstice, a curious alignment occurs. During these two days, a shaft of light stretches from one doorway to the other in the largest mound, signaling the midpoints of the solar annual cycle, or yearly calendar. The corner doorway also lines up with the Hole in the Rock, a natural feature in the nearby Papago Buttes to the northeast that may have served as a prehistoric astronomical observatory.

There is a mysterious maze within the compound. Restricted entryways and the layout of the rooms make it appear to be a purposeful labyrinth with three-foot-high walls constructed of adobe. The maze of rooms contained fascinating artifacts leading to speculation that it was a sacred site. Could this have been where feasts were prepared, and secret activities carried out?

In the late 1980s, archaeologists discovered a group of clay figures in the form of seven dogs about four to five inches tall below the soil of the floor in the Hohokam pit house. Why they were carved and what they were used for remain a mystery, but some believe they were used as part of a fertility ritual.

The mysterious maze within the Pueblo Grande Ruins compound. *Author's collection.*

These days, visitors can venture out on a fully accessible two-third-mile trail that takes them though the prehistoric Hohokam archaeological village site with a partially excavated platform mound, ball court and replicated prehistoric houses.

Local Native Americans believe this is a very spiritual place. If you are open and listen closely, you are almost certain to encounter the faint echo of Hohokam spirits of the past.

Pueblo Grand Ruins
4619 East Washington Street
Phoenix, AZ 85034

First Baptist Church

The First Baptist Church was built in 1929. While local architects Lee Mason Fitzhugh and Lester A. Byron were the masterminds, preparing the working drawings and supervising the building's construction, it was primarily designed by supervising architect George Merrill of the Department of Architecture of the American Baptist Home Mission Society in New York.

It was meticulously designed in an Italian Gothic style but includes Moderne and other architectural elements of its day with its clean lines and large porthole window, but with less filigree than one would imagine in a Gothic church. It boasted stone columns, Italian Gothic details and arched doorways.

In the 1920s, a Baptist congregation of about two thousand members pledged money to build a majestic church on Third Avenue and Monroe Street in booming downtown Phoenix. A new facility was in demand when the earlier church became too small for its expanding congregation. The congregation's first downtown church was located at Second Avenue and Jefferson Street. It burned down in a fire.

The debut of the New First Baptist Church building began on April 2, 1930, with three pre-dedication events. Alexander Schreiner of Salt Lake City, Utah, presented an organ recital. An informal reception for members of various Baptist churches was held on April 3, and a special dedication of the church organ was held on April 4.

"This was finished in 1929, just before the Depression. It was a big church; 1,400 or more people were here for services. It was designed for chorale singing and mass choirs," said Terry Goddard, former Arizona attorney general and the self-proclaimed protector of the church. After forty glorious years, the organ was unplugged, and the hymns were silenced as the congregation packed up and moved out, leaving the large structure abandoned. A new church was built in a more suburban Phoenix neighborhood.

Tragedy overcame the vacant building in the 1980s. The historic Phoenix church was destroyed by fire in the early hours of February 1984. The fire was reported at 5:10 a.m. by a passing taxi driver. At 5:23 a.m., most of the roof of the sanctuary collapsed, so firefighters spent most of their time battling the blaze from the outside of the building. The rest of the roof crumbled piece by piece. The fire was contained by 6:39 a.m. The church looked as though an atom bomb had been dropped on it, creating a perfect setting for an old horror movie.

The downtown fire caused an estimated $500,000 in damage to the former church. The building's three-story sanctuary fell deep into the basement, bringing the balcony and stage crashing down to ground zero. The blaze displaced about a dozen transients who had found shelter for warmth and had been sleeping in the building illegally. The transients smelled smoke for at least two hours but believed it was just one of many small heating fires.

The fire sent flames higher than the building's six-story bell tower. Transients scrambled out of windows and doors, according to fire officials. No injuries were reported. Eleven transients living in the building were interviewed by local police. Some said a man known only as "Wolf" didn't make it out. They noted that he was last seen going down to the basement to grab some of his belongings.

The sanctuary was destroyed inside, but the four outer concrete walls remained standing. The church had no roof, which left it looking like a majestic ruin. Gone was the ornate, circular stained-glass window that served as a focal point. Gone were the ornate, stained-glass windows over the entrance. The blaze did not burn the offices and classrooms next to the sanctuary, but the rooms suffered smoke and fire damage. Before the fire, plans had been made to turn the building into an office space called "The Abbey."

A nonprofit group, Housing Opportunity Center, wished to redevelop the church into affordable housing apartments. Former Phoenix mayor Terry Goddard, who represented the group, saved the building from the wrecking ball by offering to buy it at a rock-bottom price, and a deal was finally arranged.

Goddard said, "The church is a gorgeous building and very important to the history of Phoenix. Besides, I take an interest in it because it burned on the third day that I was named the mayor."

For over twenty years, this forty-thousand-square-foot building has been transformed into an open-air sanctuary for thousands of birds and nearly fifty thousand honey bees who tried to build their hives up within the old rose windows. Local architects continue to design plans to renovate the structure. Some envision the main sanctuary as a beautiful garden setting or an open-air concert venue beneath the starry Arizona skies.

The building has been in the National Historic Register of Historic Places since 1982.

In recent years, artist Robert John Miley converted the space in the old rectory as his imaginative studio. He is known for his work of art *Release the Fear—Melted Weapons Sculpture*. Erected in a small Phoenix park, it is composed of eight and a half tons of metal, eight thousand pounds of which were salvaged from weapons used in violent acts throughout Arizona.

It was in his studio that Miley had a paranormal experience he could not explain. He was looking to expand his workspace and spent an afternoon

Gloomy ruins of a 1984 fire remain at the First Baptist Church. *Author's collection.*

exploring various hidden alcoves within the building. He climbed on a stepladder and began to look for old treasures that might have been hidden or stored away for decades. He looked down and saw a small child—a young girl who reminded him of actress Shirley Temple. She had golden curls and wore a fancy party dress and black patent leather shoes. Her image seemed real, and for a moment, Miley wondered how the little girl was able to enter his studio. For a moment, the spirit from another dimension and Miley became one on this planet, with their eyes locked on each other. She gazed up at him, smiled, then slowly faded away, disappearing back to another place in time. Was the girl a former member of the First Baptist Church? Did she die many years ago at a tender age and was brought to the church for a funeral celebration of her life? We may never know the answers.

First Baptist Church
302 West Monroe Street
Phoenix, AZ 85003

GEORGE WASHINGTON CARVER MUSEUM AND CULTURAL CENTER

The George Washington Carver Museum and Cultural Center is housed in an early historic Phoenix high school building. When the school opened in 1926, it was known as Phoenix Union Colored High School, a segregated school for African Americans in the Phoenix metro area. However, the name was changed to George Washington Carver High School in 1943—the year of Carver's death.

The school was built on the site of a former four-acre landfill and was surrounded by small factories and warehouses. In the beginning, there were protests to the location, since it was so close to the industrial and contaminated area. Phoenix physicians feared the site was a "hot bed and nucleus of virulent contagious diseases."

Carver High School began as the only educational option for black students. The school turned out to be a first-rate educational institution because of the great quality and motivation of the teachers and staff. The classmates were inspired to always do their best. The school population continued to grow. Carver was remodeled and enlarged in 1948, which included new shop facilities and a one-thousand-seat stadium. The students of Carver became inspiring scholars, athletes and artists.

In 1953, an Arizona court ruled school segregation to be unconstitutional. Carver's students were integrated into other existing Phoenix high schools. Carver closed its doors as a high school in 1954. The once busy halls became a cold and dreary storage building for the Phoenix school district until 1991. The building would have been demolished had it not been for a group of alumni who banded together to save their school.

The building, and the almost five acres of land it sits on, was honored and listed in the National Register of Historic Places in 1991. The parking lot and sports stadium remain silent, but the academic building is again filled with voices and laughter. These days, the offices and classrooms have been converted into various galleries. One room commemorates the Buffalo Soldiers. Another room is filled with Carver Monarchs athletic photos, trophies and newspaper clippings.

The current board president of the George Washington Carver Museum and Cultural Center noted that when the property was under construction in 1925, there was a caretaker house built on the site. It is assumed by the board members and volunteers that the spirit of the caretaker has remained behind to watch over the property. The reports from the group state his presence has been felt at various areas on the old school grounds. Folks often

A George Washington Carver statue graces the old 1926 high school. *Courtesy of Wikimedia.*

have a feeling of being watched by a protective gentleman, but when they look around, no one is there…or is he?

George Washington Carver once said: "Anything will give up its secrets if you love it enough. Not only have I found that when I talk to the little flower or to the little peanut, they will give up their secrets, but I have also found that when I silently commune with people, they give up their secrets also—if you love them enough."

George Washington Carver Museum and Cultural Center
415 East Grant Street
Phoenix, AZ 85004

WESTWARD HO HOTEL

The Westward Ho opened its doors on November 1928 at its location along Central and Fillmore Streets and was the toast of the town for many years until its official closure as a guest hotel in April 1980. It held the title of the tallest building in Phoenix for over thirty years until the completion of the Meridian Bank Tower in 1960. Construction of the hotel was announced in spring 1927 under the originally planned name, the Roosevelt Hotel. The project was financed by Sutherlin-Barry & Company of New Orleans, Louisiana, for owner G.L. Johnson. The architectural team that designed the elegant Spanish-influenced Art Deco hotel building was Fisher, Lake and Traver, which had also designed the Roosevelt Hotel in Hollywood, California, a few years before.

Several famous people stayed at the hotel, which boasted sixteen floors and a patio annex. Among the renowned guests and personalities were the following: John F. Kennedy, Ronald Reagan, Paul Newman, Elizabeth Taylor, Nicky Hilton, Roy Rogers, Tom Mix, the Marx Brothers, Jackie Gleason, Myrna Loy, Mae West, Esther Williams, Danny Thomas, Gary Cooper, Lucille Ball, Clark Gable, Henry Fonda, Ava Gardner, Bob Hope, Liberace, Lee Marvin, Tyrone Power, Eleanor Roosevelt, Eddie Fisher, Shirley Temple, Al Capone, Bugsy Siegel, Irving Berlin, Duke Ellington, Spencer Tracy and John Wayne. Actor Robert Wagner married Natalie Wood out on the hotel patio. Amelia Earhart was not a movie star, a millionaire or a gangster; however, she did stay at the Westward Ho before her plane mysteriously vanished in 1937.

President John F. Kennedy stayed in one of the patio suites while recovering from injuries he suffered in World War II. It is speculated that he romanced Marilyn Monroe in his secluded suite: Room 218. The Westward Ho was one of his favorite locations in Phoenix, and he once delivered a campaign speech from the steps of the east entrance.

In September 1941, the Westward Ho was the scene of a robbery. The lucky bandits were able to make a fast getaway! Two bandits, one of them disguised with actors' greasepaint, held up the Westward Ho Hotel and escaped with more than $300. Three desk clerks and an employee of the hotel garage were herded behind a counter as the pair, brandishing pistols, ransacked the cash drawer. The four employees reported to police that one of the holdup men threatened to kill Clark Ferrill, the night clerk, because he couldn't open the office safe. The younger of the two gunmen, about twenty-eight years old, had a villainous appearance caused by liberal use of greasepaint. His eyebrows were said by the victims to have been smeared with black paint, and he had a carefully designed grease mustache. The rest of his face was covered with an orange-flesh coating. The other bandit, about thirty-two, had a swarthy complexion with several days' growth of beard.

Then, in May 1947, one of the guests began to run amuck from within the swank hotel. Harry R. Sime, forty-eight, of Glendale, California, was jailed pending charges of firing eight wild shots in the Westward Ho and leading the police on a twenty-minute chase over stairs and fire escapes before his capture.

Injured by a blow to his head during the affair was Herman Cohn, forty-six, a legal investor and collector. Police said Cohn was threatened by Sime and forced at gunpoint down eleven flights of stairs at the hotel, struck on the head and in the ribs with the weapon and forced to jump to the ground from a second-floor fire escape extension ladder.

Cohn told police he met Sime in the cocktail lounge and went with him and several others to a room on the thirteenth floor, where they had a drink or two. A few minutes later, Sime started shooting and marched Cohn down stairs and fire escapes.

The investigation disclosed that one shot had been fired in Sime's room and seven others in the hotel corridors. One of the shots passed through the door of a room in which a man and his wife were sleeping. Sime finally surrendered to police on a second-floor fire escape. Cohn went to a Phoenix hospital, where four stitches were needed to close the two-inch scalp laceration he received.

Another bizarre tale, in October 1975, caused the streets near the Westward Ho to be torn up when Phoenix police went on a treasure hunt for $53,000 in stolen jewels! The dig produced only a twelve-foot trench across a nearby street.

Police sergeant John Roberts said the object of the search was jewelry heisted in 1958 from the walk-in vault at the Hotel Westward Ho. Roberts said a boy may have buried the stolen loot years ago. Agents of the insurance firm, which long ago paid off the loss, watched anxiously as a backhoe ripped open the earth. But, alas, there were no jewels. Roberts said the stones may have been found earlier, it could have been the wrong spot or there may have been nothing buried there in the first place.

Victim of the theft was Lothar Gates of Yonkers, New York, who arrived in Phoenix on October 17, 1958, with two sample cases of jewelry. He called on several dealers that day, then took the cases to the hotel, placing them in the Westward Ho vault. The next morning, the cases were gone. Gates, cleared of any implication in the theft after a lie detector test, maintained his employment by the firm.

Roberts said police later learned that a twelve-year-old boy saw a big black car drive to the eastside location. A man jumped out and hid two cases in the brush. The boy took the cases home, only to discover a glittering collection of ruby rings, diamonds and bracelets packed within.

Roberts said the youngster, unwilling to report his find, decided to bury the cases, carefully noting the spot. Soon afterward, he moved to California with his family. Roberts said the boy, who was twenty-nine years old when he returned to Phoenix, found the spot covered by a new street. He told his tale to another man, who reported it to Roberts's nephew in Phoenix.

"We didn't know whether to believe the story or not," said Roberts. "But everything that could be researched did match the description of the two cases, and the missing jewelry. Even the time period seems to be right."

The young man who supposedly buried the jewelry as a boy is still unidentified. Roberts says he has no solution, but more digging doesn't seem to be the answer.

"I'd sure hate to see them dig up the whole street, especially since the stuff may never have been buried there in the first place." I guess you could say the Phoenix treasure hunt was a bust!

The hotel is now used for the elderly and disabled and as low-income housing. Each resident resides in a self-contained apartment. Although talk of the paranormal among residents is discouraged, many of the longtime dwellers have experienced paranormal phenomena from time to time.

In September 2001, psychic Jackie Kranz and I were invited by the Historical Committee Team of the Westward Ho Hotel to take a personal tour of the facility led by Earling Eaton. This was a special treat for Jackie, as she worked her first job at the hotel as a waitress in the soda fountain during her teen years. This has always kept the hotel near and dear to her heart.

"The fountain closed shortly after I left my job there—I think I was about sixteen years old. The year had to be 1966. I met my first husband while working there."

Earling acquired a set of keys and opened locked doors that led to the basement. He showed us the tunnels that once ran under busy Central Avenue to an adjacent parking lot. The tunnels were later closed off and collapsed during the construction of the Phoenix Valley Metro Light Rail. I wanted to venture into the dark tunnel system but was warned that transients sometimes made their home in the tunnels because of the cooler

Westward Ho Hotel was once a busy resort visited by dignitaries and movie stars. *Author's collection.*

temperatures. I was satisfied to snap a few photos in the doorway before we closed and secured the heavy door.

"Speaking of tunnels," Jackie giggled. "There was supposed to be a tunnel that had caved in where an old Model T, or a car was hidden away—and it was said to belong to a famous gangster." The Westward Ho was one of the few resort hotels in the Phoenix, Arizona area. It was quite elaborate for its day. Many of the people who stayed there were movie stars, and the guest list also included notorious gangsters. The tunnel system under the hotel was rumored to be a quick getaway if necessary. One tunnel went under Central Avenue, and another tunnel traveled below Fillmore and into another building across the street below the present United States Post Office. Some say the post office was built on the grounds where the home of an early Phoenix judge once stood. Another rumor stated that the judge used the tunnels to visit the underground speakeasy of the Westward Ho during Prohibition. Can you guess which speakeasy avoided being raided?

Exploring the vast basement, we visited the dressing rooms and lockers where staff changed into crisp uniforms and prepared for another day's work—all bringing back happy memories for Jackie. She looked at a wall and noticed an old framed set of the hotel blueprints that staff officials had long forgotten until that moment.

Earling ushered us through the passageway that led behind the stage of the Thunderbird Ballroom. There were more vacant dressing rooms where bandleaders, iconic movie stars and Broadway players prepared for shows and special events. Mirrors encircled with broken light bulbs hovered over dressing-room tables covered with dust. What a treat it was to explore backstage of the ghostly silent-theater ballroom.

Two months later, the MVD Ghostchasers held one of their first paranormal workshops at the Westward Ho location. The event doubling as a fundraiser for the Westward Ho Historic Committee, the MVD Ghostchasers invited fifty-four guests and raised $600 toward the hotel museum. They also filled two grocery carts with canned goods for the Westward Ho's resident pantry. The hotel was ecstatic, for now they would not have to buy any canned goods for the rest of the winter and residents were going to have plenty to eat for Thanksgiving and Christmas holidays.

The staff was eager to escort the workshop crew on a history tour of the Phoenix landmark. They told the visitors stories and showed them where the stars romped and celebrated in Phoenix's progressive years. They had tales of adventures concerning the various lounges and ballrooms where the elite mingled during the years when the Westward Ho was the playground of Phoenix society.

The workshop participants broke up into three groups, but everyone attending the event was able to visit the Concho Room, the pool and garden, the Kachina Lounge and the spacious lobby—including the staircase where it is said Roy Rogers road his horse, Trigger, down the steps. They also gazed upon the large wooden doors of the 19th Hole Lounge, the beautiful Turquoise Room with its real inlaid turquoise mosaic flooring tiles, the spacious Thunderbird Ball Room (scene of many a prom and wedding reception) and the isolated Garden Deck on the fifteenth floor that connected to the Presidential Suite.

"We went into the Concho room where my father used to work as a bartender," Jackie recalled. "And if you remember, my daughter was with me, who has never met my father. We could actually hear people singing in the Concho room to music. It was amazing! Everyone at the event heard the voices, too!"

The most oppressive zone of the hotel was the penthouse area on the fifteenth floor. Several of the investigators sensed there was once a brutal fight or accident on the Garden Deck. In fact, as one of the investigators walked through the Garden Deck room, he stopped in his tracks and grabbed his cheek. The seasoned ghost hunter announced that it felt as though he had walked into the middle of a fistfight and was slapped by some unseen force. He had to sit down and catch his breath. Others described the area as a sad, depressing space and avoided the spot.

"The owners of the hotel resided in the penthouse for many years," Jackie nodded her head. "Yes, the penthouse was full of tension the night we investigated up there. We all could feel the uncomfortable feelings it brought on nearly everyone. I had a very uneasy feeling exploring the Garden Deck, too. I just wanted to go back downstairs."

Throughout all of Westward Ho's history of paranormal activity, no benevolent spirits have been observed or heard. The one exception is the fifteenth floor, which is locked to all but the staff. That floor housed several restaurants between 1928 and the late 1970s. Its last incarnation was "Top of the Ho." In one corner is a stairway from the fourteenth floor. The service elevator came up from the banquet kitchen on the ground floor. The elevator ended on the fourteenth floor; waiters would take up special meals to the restaurant. Sensitive people and psychics believe someone was violently attacked or murdered near the exit of that stairway. Whatever the case may be, a presence lives on, and many guests and employees feel uncomfortable near that spot.

From time to time, there are stories of ominous feelings by residents who try to go up to that floor. The elevator is not supposed to stop there anymore—but sometimes it does. The door will open, but everything is locked up. There is really nothing to look at up there except a gorgeous view of the city—and a couple of very unsettled spirits.

About five or six decades ago, a dentists' convention was being held in Phoenix. A dentist and his wife went to see a movie at the old Fox Theatre on Washington Street. Halfway through the movie, the wife excused herself to go to the restroom. While her husband waited, she calmly walked north on Central Avenue to the Westward Ho, took the elevator to the fifteenth floor and jumped out of the window. Nobody knew why. After that, the windows were secured so a tragedy like that could never happen again.

Some of the more intuitive investigators at the hotel felt the presence of dancing guests in the ballroom. The most famous spirit at the Ho is the "Lady in the Red Dress," who has been seen dancing next to the stage in the old Thunderbird Room. Back in the hotel days, this was the huge room where meetings, banquets, dances and various other entertainment events were held.

A more recent visit in 2012 showed off some of the improvements made in the hotel. The once empty Thunderbird Ballroom has now been split into two floors and converted into thirty-two modern apartments. When the ballroom was eliminated to provide more housing, the residents began to wonder what would happen to the dancing lady. They did not have to wait long. The ghostly dancer is still haunting the new apartments near the area where the ballroom stage once stood. The residents see her whirling, twirling residual energy passing through their rooms as though the old dance floor was still there. One second-floor, J-Wing male resident witnessed the lady in the red dress walk full figured through his apartment wall and exit into the hallway through a closed door.

Many of the residents hear the chattering of a room full of people as if a banquet or convention was back in session. Sometimes, they still hear the big-band music of Red Nichols and his Five Pennies. Red and the band often stayed and played for guests at the Westward Ho in the 1940s.

Other residents stated that kitchen utensils moved around, a stove turned itself on as a resident watched and large boxes moved themselves around noisily at night. Workmen avoided entering a particular storeroom because of odd happenings while the new apartment units were being constructed.

In 2008, following the passing of a resident on the second floor, a young woman who was packing up the belongings repeatedly saw a thin, older lady in a fancy blue gown accompanying her in the rooms. As she packed for several hours, the music from the 1940s kept playing in the background and included occasional pops that were typical of old records on a Victrola. She also heard the chatter of a room full of people—the sound of a noisy night club. The same full-length apparition in blue, complete with similar music and crowd sounds, was seen in 2009 and 2010 by two other residents, who had no idea of their same experience.

A former female security guard stopped by the Westward Ho and pointed up to the building's marquee. "I worked here two years ago as a guard."

One night, she was sent to check out a call from the thirteenth floor. Her muscles froze as she attempted to leave the elevator. Everything went limp, and she could not move. Finally, the elevator doors shut and the car headed to another floor. A few weeks later, she went down the stairs to the basement below the Thunderbird Annex. When she reached the bottom floor, two unseen hands grasped her shoulders and would not let her proceed any farther. Similar things happened years earlier in the dressing room behind the old stage.

A gentleman who lived on the third floor in the Tower building used to sit—sometimes for hours—on the edge of his bed for many years. When he passed away, a new tenant acquired his apartment. She noted that she could often see someone sitting on the edge of her bed. She asked her neighbors if anyone had died in that apartment recently. They nodded yes and asked her to describe what she saw. Without any coaxing or prompting, the new tenant described the former resident to a T.

In December 2011, a report came in regarding a haunted closet on the seventh floor. A visiting six-year-old grandson refused to enter his grandmother's closet to get something she needed. When asked why, he assured her he was not afraid of the dark. He was not claustrophobic. He simply felt uncomfortable when "another little boy's voice" in the closet said, "Talk to me." They did not know the name of the little boy in the closet. Perhaps someday, a visiting guest will take a few minutes to talk back to him and find the answer.

A curious resident at the Westward Ho began to record the hauntings and tales he heard from various folks living at the facility. Some of the spirit behaviors seem repetitive and overlapped in many of the floors and rooms. Phenomena witnessed by several people and groups over the years include visual and audio instances, manipulation of solid and liquid matter and cold breezes that occurred during the sightings.

One of the greatest myths about the Westward Ho is that Al Capone's car—full of cash and treasures—is buried in the basement. Capone did frequent the hotel in the late 1920s through 1931. Until Prohibition ended in 1933, the hotel reportedly had a speakeasy located in a secret, second basement that was not indicated on any architectural plans. It had no structural reason to exist. The basement was and still is an immense structure that once contained a bowling alley, a large underground parking garage and locker rooms for the employees. Visitors could also park on the ground level lot on the east side of Central Avenue and walk underground to the Ho. Roy Rogers even drove his horse trailer underground—presumably—since he rode Trigger up the stairs to the lobby. Part of the hotel's basement collapsed during a rainstorm in 1935—long after Capone surrendered to the grand jury in 1931. Whatever was in the collapsed section of the basement, it was never excavated. Apparently, there was still room to park other cars. Was there really a speakeasy in the secret second basement? One gentleman said he once peered into a subterranean room, lowering a camera probe through cracks of a metal trapdoor. He could see a table and a bed and electrical or water pipes running across a wall. He tried to find that trapdoor on a later date with no success.

The Westward Hotel had a fascinating female resident the other dwellers called "Scotty." She lived to be about 108 years old and claimed to be the cook for Al Capone during Prohibition days. She acknowledged that gangsters really did carry tommy guns in violin cases. She saw it all!

Since the Westward Ho is a secured private home for many of its residents, there are no ghost hunts or tours available. You can visit the hotel only if you are family or are personally invited by one of the permanent residents.

Westward Ho Hotel
618 North Central Avenue
Phoenix, AZ 85004

2
OLD WAREHOUSE DISTRICT

PHOENIX UNION STATION

The Phoenix Union Station was completed in 1923 by the Santa Fe and Arizona Eastern (Southern Pacific) Railroads. The station is a great example of Mission Revival architecture, which was very popular between 1890 and the 1920s in the Southwest.

It was constructed with a central two-story waiting room situated between two long, low arcaded wings. The stucco wall building was topped with a red-tiled roof, curvilinear gables, massive piers and impost moldings. The waiting room had a high, beamed space with wooden furnishings and chandelier ceiling light fixtures.

It still has the penny-tile bathrooms, and a carved oak refreshment counter is tucked in a corner with an idle icebox still intact. The once-bustling ticket booths stand erect with circa 1923 luggage carts stored nearby.

Phoenix Union Station was served by as many as eighteen trains a day when rail travel was at its peak during and immediately after World War II. It was the spot where servicemen kissed their gals goodbye before heading off to war. A couple of Santa Fe trains arrived and departed for Parker, Barstow and Los Angeles. The Southern Pacific line operated the Sunset Limited between Los Angeles and New Orleans.

The station played host to many special occasions and celebrations. The two events with the largest record attendance was the Main Line celebration

Phoenix Union Station was opened in 1923. *Courtesy of Wikimedia.*

on October 15, 1926, and the second day of Phoenix Union Pacific Days on February 24, 1991. On both dates, more than ten thousand people came together to celebrate the importance of the historic station and the invaluable served it provided throughout its years.

Phoenix Union Station was the center of the news in 1931, when the "trunk murderess," Winnie Ruth Judd, packed her former roommates into two large trunks and a hatbox and had them loaded onto the train as cargo.

On the evening of October 16, 1931, a Phoenix secretary by the name of Winnie Ruth Judd had an argument with her two best friends. All three of them were seeking affection from the same married man. That night, Judd shot both ladies, carved one of them up in pieces and placed both bodies into large steamer trunks, which she brought to Union Station as baggage, bound for Los Angeles.

When Judd arrived in Los Angeles, she went to claim her trunks. But, with a twist of fate, the porter had already flagged them and demanded a key to look inside, thinking there was illegal deer meat transported over the state line. Winnie Ruth Judd's trunks were leaking and oozing with blood.

Phoenix's "trunk murderess" was arrested, convicted and served over thirty-nine years in prisons and insane asylums. The bodies of Judd's friends were sent back to Phoenix on the Golden State Limited. They arrived on October 24 on the 7:20 a.m. train to Phoenix Union Station.

Until outdated by Phoenix Sky Harbor International Airport in the 1950s, Phoenix Union Station was the undisputed gateway into downtown Phoenix. The station made a comeback as an Amtrak station until the routes were rescheduled through Maricopa and Flagstaff. Don't show up at Union Station today expecting to board a train. The last Amtrak train stopped at Union Station in 1995.

In 1996, the Olympic Torch Train stopped here twice, and tourist trains such as the Grand Luxe (formerly the Orient Express) have graced the rails at the station.

Today, visitors are no longer welcomed at the station. Fences, locks and gates were placed on the property shortly after the last passenger moved on. Sprint Communications now owns the building and stores equipment that connects several of the communication networks.

The old Phoenix Union Station boasts of a ghost that security guards have nicknamed "Fred." The station's security guard/maintenance man insists that "whenever you are up in the attic of the station, and you feel a tap on your shoulder, and you turn around to find no one is there—that is Fred!" Some maintenance workers and repairmen refuse to go into the attic alone.

Fred has been known to open and close the heavy side gate or appear as a shadow figure at the other end of the room. The security guard has seen somebody running across the floor, knowing he was the only person in the building. He has felt Fred looking over his shoulder, which immediately gave him a chill.

But who is Fred? A former railroad station employee? A frequent traveler? Or perhaps an early Phoenix citizen who just liked being there? The security guard joked that the name *Fred* just came to him one day—and that is how Fred became the "ghost of Union Station."

The security guard claims he is a skeptic, and he stands firm with never allowing a paranormal investigation inside the train station. And many a reputable paranormal team has tried to make its way inside past the wire fence and barbed wire.

But! A communications class from Scottsdale Community College made arrangements with its department for a special tour. The students were there to study the vast communications wire system in the building and the art décor long forgotten. A group of female students asked to be excused and

The last Amtrak train stopped at Union Station in 1995. *Author's collection.*

use the restroom on the ground floor. The giggling group of coeds walked together to the facilities. The rest of the students heard loud shrieking screams as the ladies ran back out in terror to the lobby, where their classmates stood in terror.

"There was a man standing in the restroom!," one of the girls cried.

The male instructor and the men in the group, along with the security guard, dashed into the restroom to confront the intruder. The brave men swung open the bathroom door to find no one in sight. There was no way anyone could have entered or exited the room without observation by the visiting group.

"Must have been Fred," the security man declared.

Phoenix Union Station remains closed. The travelers by train have been derailed, although millions of voices travel via the communications network of cables that flow through the annex. The excitement of train travel has been silenced, and perhaps the only ones who can still hear the ghostly train whistle in the night are spirits just like Fred.

Phoenix Union Station
401 South Fourth Avenue
Phoenix, AZ 85003

SANTA FE FREIGHT DEPOT

Just down the track from the Phoenix Union Station stands the Santa Fe
Freight Depot. The reinforced poured concrete freight house shares a hint
of the art deco modern design that was so popular in 1929. The building
held freight offices in charge of handling large baggage and documenting
incoming and outgoing freight. The outside walls are highlighted with a few
cast Santa Fe Railroad emblems.

Situated on the southwest corner of Fifth Avenue and Jackson Street, the
15,000-square-foot building opened its doors in 1929. It was constructed by
the Atchison, Topeka and Santa Fe Railroad companies and conveniently
located where the Santa Fe and Southern Pacific tracks met—the only place

The Santa Fe Freight Depot features an art deco design, popular in 1929. *Author's collection.*

in Arizona where the two major railroads were connected. The warehouse district thrived because of the importance of this connection point.

It provided a depot where there was an easy transfer of goods, and it was convenient for Winnie Ruth Judd to have those oversized trunks delivered and weighed before being loaded on the Southern Pacific train bound for Los Angeles.

For decades, the depot was a hub of freight traffic for Phoenix and included underground tunnels connected to the nearby Icehouse, which provided cold ice in order to keep food fresh during transit. It was refurbished to serve as headquarters for the Maricopa County Assessor's Offices.

Phoenix's "Hip Historian" Marshall Shore retained an office space in the Icehouse across the street from the Santa Fe Depot building. One afternoon, an employee for the Maricopa County Assessor's Office noticed Shore unloading supplies from his vehicle and walked across the street to introduce himself.

"You're Marshall Shore, that guy they call the 'Hip Historian,' right?" the county employee inquired.

"Indeed!" Shore offered a handshake.

"If you have a few minutes, I have a story for your Haunted Phoenix Bus Tour," the man said, pointing to his watch.

The two men found a shady spot to chat, and Marshall Shore quickly pulled out a small notepad to jot down the exciting information.

"Well, a few years ago I was here working late with one of my coworkers. It started raining very hard. Streets were flooding, water was gushing down the streets—you know, one of the one-hundred-year floods we somehow get about every twenty years."

They both laughed.

"Well, I knew the streets were going to be flooded with water and traffic would be a mess, so I insisted that my coworker should leave and get a head start on the weather and go home. I still had a small project to finish and didn't live too far way, so I knew I could tough it out a while longer. She was relieved and didn't hesitate to leave."

Shore could tell by the look in the county worker's eyes that he was about to share a tale he did not tell many acquaintances, for fear of being made fun of. Nor did he have any explanation for what he experienced.

"So, I was sitting there all alone working on my computer when all of a sudden I hear a manual typewriter clicking away in the distance. Now when was the last time you have heard or even seen one of those old-fashioned manual typewriters *anywhere*?"

"Not since I visited my grandmother when I was in grade school!" Shore responded.

"Me either," he chuckled. "I stood up and started checking every nook of the building. The typewriting kept clicking away as though a baggage freight clerk from the past was preparing freight invoices for the old Santa Fe Depot. And then it suddenly stopped. And, I was out of there! I have never heard it again—just that one stormy evening. Please feel free to use this anecdote on your tour!"

And Marshall Shore did just that! It has been one of the favorite stories on his two-hour haunted history bus tour through the city of Phoenix.

Santa Fe Depot
334 South Fifth Avenue
Phoenix, AZ 85003

ARVIZU'S EL FRESNAL GROCERY STORE

Part of Phoenix's old warehouse district still exists between Seventh Avenue and Seventh Street, and between Madison Street and south to Grant Street. One of the most interesting—and, I must say, more mysterious—of the remaining buildings is the historic Arvizu's El Fresnal Grocery Store on Buchanan Street. It sits vacant, protected for future preservation.

It was placed in the National Register of Historic Places in 1985, but there is not much to see inside the once thriving grocery store these days. A *Phoenix New Times* reporter was able to peek in a window and noted seeing a "couple of empty, open rooms with ratty blue carpet on the floors. There were a few metal dining chairs in the front room, but no signs that it had ever been one of the popular groceries in downtown Phoenix."

The red brick building was constructed in 1900, a good twelve years before Arizona became a state. It grew to be the earliest Hispanic-owned grocery store in downtown Phoenix and was owned and operated by Señor Trinidad Arvizu from 1900 to 1920. It closed as a grocery in 1924 when the quantity of grocery stores and marketplaces had suddenly increased with the ever-growing Phoenix population.

Trinidad Arvizu was charged with the receiving of fruits of the nocturnal industry (illegal goods), including forty-four bags of stolen barley, which he knowingly resold to his friends and neighbors. He was fined eighty-eight dollars. Trinidad and his wife, Rosario Arvizu, are buried in Phoenix's Greenwood Cemetery.

Take a closer look at the building. The rickety brick structure still bears the weathered paint advertising the long-closed grocery store in bold lettering. "Ghost signs," as they call them these days.

This is a ghost story that won't keep you up all night trembling under the covers. Everyone has seen these "ghosts" at one time or another—but it probably didn't even register. There are *signs* of ghosts in almost every historic district of a town, including Phoenix. Ghost signs are merely faded advertisements on the walls of hotels or other commercial buildings. They were once as common as today's TV commercials.

Many businesses hired a sign painter, who could turn a plain red brick wall into an advertisement for hotel rooms, clothing, cigars, hardware and

The old Arvizu grocery building shared meeting space for the Masons. *Author's collection.*

more. Now all that is left of these colorful ads are white wispy spirits clinging to the decaying walls as eerie reminders of past decades.

In the heyday of building advertisements, the signs were painted by brave men known as wall dogs. They were fine artists and fearless daredevils scaling the sides of buildings—sometimes several stories high. With such a dangerous vocation, there was also an occasional accident. Do the spirits of these lost artists become one with the "ghosts" they created?

But wait! Look again. Get a little closer. As you scan the signage on the rear of the building, you will discover the hidden history embedded in the bricks—specifically, the remnant signs indicating that this was once a Mexican Masonic Temple!

We can speculate that the store doubled as a fraternal meeting place after-hours. If you look carefully, high up on the bricks, you can still see the Masonic "G" symbol, along with an upside-down, five-pointed silver star (most likely symbolizing the Eastern Star here). There is also a faded circle painted above the rear archway that was once a brilliant sun with rays.

Colleen Sulzer and I decided to take a drive to the site of the old grocery and see if the Masonic symbols were still visible to the eye. After circling the building on the one-way streets a few times, we found the perfect lighting and discovered that the "ghosts" and the memories of the old Mexican Masonic Temple were still very much "alive."

Arvizu's El Fresnal Grocery Store
310 East Buchanan Street
Phoenix, AZ 85004

The Icehouse

The Constable Ice and Fuel Company building (now known as the Icehouse) was built in 1920. Before refrigeration was prominent in Phoenix, ice was stored in this building. The Icehouse is located in the historic original townsite of the city of Phoenix near the railroad depot. The building is now a cultural center devoted to promoting the arts and humanitarian causes. Designated as a landmark with Historic Preservation, the building was listed in the National Register of Historic Places on September 4, 1985.

Work on a newer Constable Ice and Fuel Company cold storage addition began on December 16, 1921, and cost $40,000. The newer plant adjoined

Historic plaque at the early Phoenix Icehouse. *Author's collection.*

the older building to expand needed ice service. T.B. Stewart was the building contractor. The plan was to construct a two-story building with a basement. Provisions were made to add a third floor in the future. The foundation of the building was seventy feet by fifty feet. Construction throughout was reinforced concrete, making the plant absolutely fireproof.

There were ten cold storage rooms in the two-story building with no provisions made for office space, as headquarters of the firm remained in the old plant. The new building had thirty-five thousand cubic feet for cold storage space; when the third floor was added, it opened up an additional fifty-five thousand cubic feet. All rooms were cooled by a direct expansion system. An electric elevator was included in the modern equipment of the plant.

One of the features of the building was its heavy insulation against earth and outside atmospheric conditions. Five layers of concrete and cork were used to insulate against the earth. These layers ran as follows: six inches concrete, six inches clay tile, three inches concrete, four inches cork and four inches concrete. All floors and walls had four-inch cork insulation. Large blocks of ice would be hauled onto passing train cars in the era before refrigeration, keeping vital food cold for trips to the East and West.

Declaring that he suffered damages to the extent of $20,000 as the result of injuries to his right hand, received in an accident, John J. Callahan brought suit against T.B. Stewart and the Constable Ice and Fuel Company for judgement on May 9, 1920. Callahan alleged he was employed as a mechanical laborer on the hoisting apparatus at the ice company's new plant at Fourth Avenue and Jackson Street. He said that on March 4, 1920, the coil on the drum of the hoist became loose. Callahan alleged that while he was trying to fix it, the machinery started up in some manner, catching his right hand in the ropes. John J. Callahan, age sixty-three, died about five months later, on July 19, 1920, from lobar pneumonia. Does his spirit still haunt the warehouse?

Once refrigerated rail cars were developed, the Constable Ice Storage building was transformed into another kind of storage—crime storage. For many decades, the Phoenix Police Department used the building units to store crime-scene evidence. The facility was said to have held the burned-out remains of the car belonging to Don Bolles, the *Arizona Republic* reporter who was brutally murdered in an alleged mob hit in the Clarendon House Hotel parking lot while he investigated the mafia's presence in the Valley.

In 1990, the space was converted to its present use: an experimental arts wonderland. Helen Hestenes, owner and curator of the Icehouse, found raw material for creative inspiration of the arts. She played host to a wide array of guests of the Phoenix art scene. The building looked more like a gloomy fortress compound than a trendy art gallery.

Some of her art displays were a bit on the dark side. When a fellow artist's sister was kidnapped, Hestenes encouraged the artist to create a room-sized

The 1920 Constable Ice & Fuel Company stored ice before refrigeration was prominent in Phoenix. *Author's collection.*

piece as a memorial. The beautiful artwork consisted of three hundred long-stemmed roses hanging from the gallery ceiling—each rose representing a missing child. When the historic Borden Dairy in Phoenix was demolished in 1999, Hestenes decided to stage a mock funeral in the courtyard of the Icehouse, including a "grave" for the bygone creamery.

In the 1990s, guests entered through the Cathedral Room, a Gothic-looking brick chamber that has no ceiling and opens up to the sky. In an area called the Column Room, floor-to-ceiling roof supports broke up the warehouse space. She used the courtyard area to the west to show images on the three-story concrete wall during outdoor events. There was once an old metal kiddie roller coaster called the "Fear Coaster" for visitors to ride, complete with flames, lighting bolts and fake skulls.

The Icehouse began as a mecca for raves, or all-night dance parties involving drugs, drinking, sex and other dangerous lifestyle habits. There were still artists working in private studios, business proprietors renting office space and, sometimes, seedy people living in empty rooms. It was a place where runaways would hide, and one could only imagine the terror and crimes committed in the dark confines of the isolated concrete storage rooms. There were too many fire-code violations to list, including unmarked exits, insufficient fire escapes and fire extinguishers, lack of sprinklers. The place was a potential building of doom.

Renovations were made, artists began to flock back to work their magic and the Icehouse has once again become a trendy art gallery and reception hall.

But what really lurks within the cork-insulated walls? Arizona's Hip Historian, Marshall Shore, kept an office in the basement confines of the Icehouse. It was either icy cold in the winter or blistering hot in the summer, but the rent was cheap and just what he needed and could afford at the time. He invited Cindy Lee and me to take a tour of the facility as a potential spot to do a group paranormal investigation.

We began our tour outside and peeked into the storage shed where Don Bolles's 1976 Datsun sedan was hidden away and stored for the Phoenix crime lab after the deadly explosion. We went inside and walked every floor, peeking into the rooms of various galleries and noting the styles of the various artists' work. Marshall walked us into a secluded large room on the top floor and paused near the doorway.

"Do you feel anything in here?" Shore asked as Cindy and I wandered slowly in the room.

"Does not feel good," I shrugged.

Lone chair in an eerie room at the Icehouse. *Author's collection.*

"Something really bad happened in here." Cindy walked to one corner.

She stood quietly and raised her arms, trying to feel the residual energy "Something really bad happened over in this area. I feel a male energy. There were a lot of people who came up here to do drugs—maybe one overdosed or died up here. There is a very dark and negative energy lingering behind. I don't like it in here at all."

We visited the dank basement and wandered the halls of studios where some artists still create their work, but nothing seemed as menacing as the large room on the top floor.

The Crossing Over Paranormal team, led by Jay and Marie Yates, has also investigated the Icehouse. The most activity they encountered was in the Cathedral Room, the room with no ceiling. They caught a lot of EVP in the building capturing voices from the past. Jay and Marie went upstairs at separate times; both felt the sensation of being pushed. Marie was so affected by the energy that she had to come back downstairs. Jay sat in the first room upstairs to the left—what is known as the "Black Room"—and began an isolation session. As he sat there alone, he saw a shadow cross in front of the door frame with light in the hallway.

"It scared me pretty good!" Jay Yates affirmed.

A room with the swirls had a lot of intelligent responses to questions when using the REM Pod and K2 meter—yes and no answers. COPS Crew members reported seeing a shadow in that room. The group heard a lot of knocks and bangs in response to questioning in the outside evidence room.

Jay noted that he became interested in the building when he worked as a correctional officer at the Maricopa County Fourth Avenue Jail. "Several officers and myself would often hear screams coming from the building and see shadows in the upstairs windows."

There is no doubt that the shadows, screams and icy secrets could have been left in cold storage for those in the present to experience.

The Icehouse
429 West Jackson Street
Phoenix, AZ 85003

3

PHANTOMS OF THE THEATER

PHOENIX THEATRE

Phoenix Theatre was originally founded as the Phoenix Players back in 1920. It is the oldest arts organization in Arizona and believed to be one of the oldest operating arts organizations in the United States. In the early days, the Phoenix Players performed everywhere and anywhere they were welcomed, including schools and neighboring backyards. There became a need for a permanent performance theater space. In 1924, the Heard family offered the newly named Phoenix Little Theatre their old coach house on Central Avenue and McDowell Road.

In 1952, funding for the construction of a new building had begun. This building would become part of a cultural area that would welcome the Phoenix Art Museum, the Phoenix Public Library and the Phoenix Little Theatre.

Through the course of Phoenix's growth and history, Phoenix Theatre has launched careers in the industry, developed the love of theater in young audiences, introduced new playwrights and composers and hosted two world premieres.

Most American theaters have a "ghost light" that is switched on when the cast and crew have left the theater at the end of the performance each night. Sometimes, it is a simple bare light bulb on a stand, or you will find it

Phoenix Theatre is home to a spirit called "Tiny Dancer." *Author's collection.*

hanging on a cord from the overhead light fixtures. It remains on until the crew arrives the next day.

The ghost light is actually considered a safety measure to prevent accidents, such as tripping over props or falling into the orchestra pit. Others believe it is there to keep ghosts or spirits away. Some say it's to keep the ghosts happy, ensuring the theater will never grow dark. Perhaps it offers the theater ghosts company during the night. The superstitions propose justifications for the ghost light in relation to the supernatural. It is believed that every theater has a ghost, and some theaters have traditions to appease ghosts that go back in history.

Theaters are hubs of an overabundance of energy stirred up among actors, crew and audience anticipating a grand performance. Ghosts need energy to manifest and communicate, so it is no wonder that the Phoenix Theatre attracts a vast array of ghostly spirits.

Sometimes, actors, who are artistic and emotional people, will channel the spirits of the characters they portray on stage to achieve a better performance. What if, once called, that spirit from the past enjoys the environment of the theater and decides to stay? Actors enjoy their work, basking in the spotlight, often not wanting to leave it. Is that because they actually give life to their characters, resurrecting them in a way? Will today's actors be tomorrow's ghosts? And don't forget, the hundreds of guests attending the performance will be bringing their own energies. Some say a theater is like an all-you-can-eat buffet, bringing in energies both good or bad.

Like many theaters around the world, the Phoenix Theatre comes complete with its own cast of spirited ghosts.

The best-known spirit has been given the title "Mr. Electric." He has been typecast as a little old man who loves to sit on the flies (pipes) that hold up the theater lighting rails. He insists on helping the electricians by turning lights on and off without a cue.

A delicate spirit called the "Tiny Dancer" first appeared during a 2005 production of *A Chorus Line*. The petite ballerina was sighted dancing on stage among the celebrated cast.

Many theater employees have nicknamed another spirit the "Prop Master." This theater ghost likes to move articles and stage set pieces around the prop room, making it difficult to prepare the next scene. The prankster ghost has locked the busy stage crew in the prop room if things aren't going his way.

There is also the ghost of "Light Board Lenny," a spirit that has locked technicians operating the light board or spotlight out of the lighting booth—the area he seems to haunt the majority of the time.

Let's not forget poor "Freddy." The actors and crew believe Freddy is the ghost of an actor who was killed in a bicycle accident after being fired from a Phoenix Theatre production. Freddy has been known to slam doors and throw items around the upstairs room, still trying to resolve the devastating feelings of being terminated.

It is these "active imaginations and animated personalities" that keep the theater alive today.

Phoenix Theatre
100 East McDowell Road
Phoenix, AZ 85004

The Orpheum Theatre shares the marquee with Gloria Swanson, 1929. *Courtesy of the Orpheum Theatre*.

ORPHEUM THEATRE

Construction on the magnificent Orpheum Theatre began in June 1927 and was completed by 1929. The structure, designed by architects Lescher & Mahoney, with associate Hugh Gilbert, cost in the neighborhood of $750,000. It was built for theater enthusiasts J.E. Rickards and Harry Nace. It promised to be "the most beautiful playhouse west of the Mississippi." It boasts a Spanish Revival style of Spanish Baroque architecture with intricate murals and moldings, all with the intentions of giving theater patrons the impression that they were enjoying the shows alfresco—outdoors in the fresh air.

In August 1925, Rickards and Nace purchased property for a new theater at the corner of Second Avenue and Adams Street from the Phoenix Lodge of the Elks for $100,000. This new theater would join the growing list of venues owned and managed by Rickards and Nace throughout Arizona.

Opening night was billed as "The Greatest Event in Theatrical History" and resembled an Oscars ceremony. Guests included Governor Hunt, Mayor Paddock, members of various businesses and civic organizations and several Hollywood celebrities, including the guest of honor, Carl Laemmle, the president of Universal Pictures.

When entering the theater, patrons were transported "as if by Aladdin's magic carpet into a new land." Its two thousand leather-upholstered seats were surrounded by a mission garden filled with flowers, vines and bubbling, glittering fountains, all beneath a pure blue sky twinkling through the clouds floating through endless space.

This venue was originally used for vaudeville acts as part of the nationwide Orpheum Circuit. In the 1940s, the Orpheum was purchased by the Paramount Pictures chain and renamed the Paramount Theatre. It was advertised as a single-feature venue, while most of the other theaters in town showed double features. The Paramount thrived in the 1950s and early 1960s, hosting Mae West appearing in person as "Diamond Lil" and showing movies such as *The Bridge on the River Kwai* and *Psycho*.

By the mid-1960s, the downtown scene began to change. The Paramount closed in December 1967 due to declining profits and lack of parking. The Nederlander organization purchased it in 1968 and added it as a stop on the Broadway circuit. Throughout the 1960s, until its restoration, it was renamed "Palace West."

By the mid-1970s and early 1980s, the theater was leased to the enterprising local Mexican Corona family, which presented a wide variety

Mae West arrives at the Orpheum Theatre in 1933. *Courtesy of the Orpheum Theatre.*

of Hispanic events and movies. At one point, when the theater was used to show only Spanish films, all the murals and moldings were painted black. In addition to the desire to hide areas that were already in poor condition, it was thought that lavish decorations would distract moviegoers from watching the films.

After falling into disrepair for some years, the Orpheum Theatre was purchased in 1984 by the City of Phoenix. The city began a thirteen-year, $14.5 million restoration project. The Conrad Schmitt Studios created the transformation, and the Orpheum reopened on January 28, 1997, with a performance of *Hello, Dolly!* starring the grand dame Carol Channing. After the breathtaking performance, Channing, still in costume but out of character, thanked the audience for "not turning this beautiful theater into a parking lot!" It is the only remaining theater built before World War II in Phoenix.

The theater's domed ceiling is famous for its projected pure blue sky and puffy white moving clouds. Shortly before the theater auditorium lights come down, the ceiling transforms into a glorious desert sunset. When darkness fills the room, look up and marvel at the darkened sky and twinkling lights. This "crown jewel of downtown Phoenix" also boasts a magnificent "Mighty Wurlitzer Theater Organ" that rises through the

The Orpheum awaits its loyal patrons. *Author's collection.*

floor with organists that wow the audiences with their music and the acoustics of the theater.

Some guests come to the Orpheum in search of its ghosts and popular ghost tours. Joe Atredies, paranormal investigator and owner of Phoenix Ghost Tours since 2009, has led ghost tours at the Orpheum Theatre since

2014. He enjoys escorting visitors on his hour-long tour into the history and mystery of the beautiful building. His first stop is the second-story office of the original owner, Harry Nace. He died mysteriously from two gunshots, and now he is said to haunt his old workspace.

Joe said in a Fox 10 interview, "Some people have heard male voices call out to them and talk to them, and even call out their name which is probably the creepiest thing you can get!"

Every theater has a "house ghost," and the Orpheum in Phoenix is no different. Maybe it is because of all of the drama that takes place both backstage and under the bright lights on the main stage. The Orpheum has given its most popular ghost a name: Maddie, or Maggie. The female spirit wears mid-twentieth-century clothing and is often seen as a shadowy figure moving about the balcony during rehearsals and late-night performances. Various paranormal teams who have investigated the show palace have captured unexplained phenomena and shadows in photos on digital cameras. The balcony is one area of the theater where many patrons encounter the spirit of Maddie/Maggie. Others have witnessed her sitting in the back rows of the main floor. She has interrupted shows, tapped patrons on the head and dazzled guests with her ornate period clothing.

MVD Ghostchaser Cindy Lee was attending a theater show with a group of her best friends. She left her seat during intermission to use the restroom and, with her gal pals, stretch her legs in the lobby. She noted a woman standing alone near the back of the theater dressed in a lovely period gown and a large maroon hat in the *Hello, Dolly!* style, accented with large black feathers. Her styled dark hair was tucked under the hat. The woman wore a beautiful maroon gown with a matching dress coat trimmed in a black lacy brocade pattern. Cindy, who does historic reenactments herself, was curious about the costuming and the fabulous hat the mysterious woman was wearing. She decided to ask the woman for the name of her seamstress or dressmaker. Cindy casually made her way to the back of the theater auditorium to speak to the woman but watched in amazement as the lady mysteriously disappeared in front of her eyes. Cindy, who is quite intuitive, was certain the woman's name was Maggie.

In June 2015, another paranormal team, FOTOS (Friends of the Other Side), did an investigation with Phoenix Ghost Tours owner Joe Atredies and a group of City of Phoenix workers. FOTOS leader Carolee Jackson encountered the same female energy in the wide-brimmed hat in the theater balcony. Carolee picked up on the name Maddie.

Grand staircase at the majestic Orpheum Theatre. *Courtesy of the Orpheum Theatre.*

Workers in the building across the street from the Orpheum have looked out of their office windows to see a transparent lady walking through the theater on a second floor that is no longer there. You see, the atrium of today's Orpheum was once a two-story affair with business offices on a second floor that included a hallway near the set of windows. The lovely Maggie/Maddie is seen strolling along the former second-floor corridor, destroyed during renovations to give the lobby an airier feeling. Now it appears the ghostly woman is walking on air from another dimension in time.

Nobody really knows who Maddie/Maggie might be. She could possibly be a relative of theater owner and manager Harry Nace. A Maggie Nace is listed in the Phoenix census and was very involved with the Masons and the ladies of the Eastern Star. The buildings of the organization were just a couple blocks away. A stroll to the theater, with most likely an unlimited free ticket, was probably a part of her weekly schedule. Maybe she had dreams of becoming a thespian, or perhaps it was a way to escape the reality of an ever-changing world.

Some of the other spirits Carolee encountered were an older Hispanic male dressed in a white shirt with sleeves rolled, dark pants, no tie or hat, presenting himself as Gilbert. He shows himself as a shadow form and has been seen by other patrons in the past. His message was that "he loves the theater and continues to visit. Gilbert likes to keep things clean and tidy possibly following the janitorial crew around the theater."

Carolee also felt the presence of two young boys in spirit that playfully ran across the lower seat aisle while she explained to the evening's observers how a REM Pod works. Facing the stage, they disappeared at the far-left lighting alcove and exit sign.

The stage has the residual energy of two men in a down-and-out fistfight. One evening, after an Orpheum performance, the sound tech was able to capture an audio clip of the fight while he was breaking down his equipment—complete with the racket of bodies crashing to the floor, heads banging and a general ruckus. Atredies recalled reading about a fight on stage involving an orchestra drummer by the name of Fred Ice. Ice was still despondent over the death of his young bride, Joyce Ice, age eighteen, who died nearby in a Heard Building medical office during an attempted abortion. Did Ice confront the doctor accused of the crime (and later found not guilty) after an Orpheum Theater performance and thus leaving an angry residual energy to be replayed over and over again for all eternity?

In the fall of 2018, I attended a special viewing at the Orpheum of the 1925 silent film classic *The Phantom of the Opera* starring Lon Chaney. With

Spiral stairs create an interesting illusion. *Courtesy of the Orpheum Theatre.*

me were Fallon Franzen, Megan Taylor and her friend Cassie. The Silent Sunday feature was accompanied by world-renowned organist Brett Valliant with the Orpheum's mighty Wurlitzer pipe organ. As we enjoyed the preshow recital, Megan's attention zoomed to the right of the stage. She witnessed what she calls the "Grey Lady"—a ghostly woman wearing a grayish floral dress with lavender accents. She wore a cloche hat upon her head. She appeared from behind a sign, swishing her dress skirt and swaying from side to side. And in a blink of an eye, she was suddenly transported to the left side of the stage, where she twirled and then sashayed off the stage. About that same time, Cassie pointed to the stage. "You saw her, too?" Megan chuckled. Cassie nodded yes and smiled. The extra-paranormal sideshow was worth the price of admission.

Atredies reports that there is also a resident "ghost cat" from the 1920s that apparently has a life or two to play out. There are newspaper accounts of a cat that took a liking to the construction workers while they were building the theater in 1929, and they adopted it as their mascot. They even named the black-and-white feline Tom. Workmen began feeding Tom, and he explored every part of the theater—even to the "grid" floor, sixty feet above stage level. Actors regard a cat—if it's not too black—to be a good omen, and Tom was permitted to stay. Several current employees have reported encounters with perhaps this same cat. In the early 2000s, guests reported that they were hearing a cat moving around—purring and walking around where living cats cannot go! A young girl on a tour insisted she saw a cat up on the guide rails and ropes above the stage. Security guards say they hear purring and the meows and have witnessed a ghostly cat that has jumped up and knocked items to the ground. We like to think that Tom the cat must have nine lives, much like the historic Orpheum Theatre.

Orpheum Theatre
203 West Adams Street
Phoenix, AZ 85003

4
TALES FROM THE CRYPT

AN ARIZONA TOMBSTONE RESCUE

The Pioneers' Cemetery Association (PCA) in Phoenix, Arizona, received a message from a woman who had been doing a bit of antique shopping in the northern part of the state. Patty, who has since become a key member of the PMMP preservation team, told the PCA board members that she had discovered an old tombstone monument sitting in front of an antiques store and wondered if the group had a way to look up the names on the stone to learn if it belonged in an Arizona cemetery.

The members of the Pioneers' Cemetery Association researched the name and dates on the stone. Not only could they tell where the tombstone originated—they also learned that the old monument belonged in the Pioneer & Military Memorial Park (cemeteries). The tombstone for M.H. Brady had been missing from the burial grounds for over seventy years.

Being one of the members of the PCA Board of Directors, I decided the tombstone must be returned to Phoenix and placed back in the cemetery section called "City/Loosley Cemetery" as soon as possible. It was as though the ghost of Mr. Brady was calling out to me, saying, "Bring my grave marker back home!" I have become somewhat of an "Indiana Jones" or "Tomb Raider" advocate when it comes to the preservation of Arizona history and relics, so I set off to the northern hills to "make a deal with the devil"—or in this case, the antiques shop owner.

Megan Taylor and I headed to Mayer, Arizona, thinking the four-foot obelisk monument would fit in the back of Megan's PT Cruiser. After making a crocodile tearful transaction with the shop owner, we came to the reality that the gravestone, weighing over five hundred pounds, was not going to budge without the aid of a tripod. We headed back to Phoenix empty-handed and began to work on plan B.

Plan "B" meant that Kenton Moore and I had to load up the engine hoist in the back of a trailer and haul it up north with his truck. The following morning, we were back on the road and headed up to Mayer once again. When we arrived at the antiques shop, I carefully wrapped the fragile treasure in mover's blankets, quilts and a wool blanket. Then it was secured onto a dolly. Meanwhile, Kenton assembled the engine hoist and prepared to load the tombstone into the back of his pickup truck.

Carefully, we raised the wrapped mummy and guided it slowly into the pickup bed. It was laid securely on cushioned drop cloths. We disassembled the engine hoist and departed for Phoenix and the old Pioneer & Military Memorial Park (cemetery). The recovery of the tombstone turned out to be a twofold bonanza! There were two names on the stone: M.J. Brady and Joe Brady.

Arriving in the parking lot of the old cemetery, Kenton began to dread having to set up the engine hoist for the second time. I looked around the cemetery and noticed that the nearby archaeological dig crew was hard at work on the Hohokam village site. Earlier that month, Hohokam relics and pit houses were discovered when a street was under construction for a new sewer line. I was able to gather about eight members of the dig crew to come to the cemetery gate and help unload the precious cargo.

We wheeled the monument inside the gates and uncovered the historic tombstone. The "Indiana Jones" dig crew was in awe at this modern-day archaeological find. So was the rest of the Pioneers' Cemetery Association members when they came to do their volunteer work the following Thursday.

I envisioned the ghosts of the old Pioneer & Military Memorial Park (cemetery) dancing in celebration that evening, welcoming the long-lost tombstone back home where it belonged. Amazingly, it was discovered that M.J. Brady's corpse had been robbed once before. Brady, a grocer in Phoenix, had a habit of sleeping with his daily earnings in a buckskin money pouch under his pillow. On the morning he passed away, his wife called in the neighbors, and soon the room was filled with a curious throng. After the coroner's jury viewed the body, she searched under the pillow for the

The Brady tombstone is safe in the PMMP cemeteries. *Author's collection.*

money pouch and found it was gone. The family had no clue which one of the curious onlookers had slipped their hand under the pillow and snatched the pouch. Like they say, "If Brady were alive today, he'd be turning over in his grave!"

HOHOKAM DIG: THE REAL GHOSTS OF PIONEER & MILITARY MEMORIAL PARK

The volunteers at the Pioneer & Military Memorial Park (cemetery) witnessed a hands-on archaeological dig on Madison Street—between Fifteenth and Thirteenth Avenues—in Phoenix, Arizona, during the months of October and November 2010. The City of Phoenix initiated a plan for major underground storm sewer drain construction at the location. Shortly after the street was trenched, historic Hohokam relics began to surface. Due to findings of Hohokam artifacts and dwellings in the past, a group of archaeologists were sent to the scene to gather samples of artifacts and to document and photograph the pit houses before the sewer construction could proceed.

This ghostly Hohokam settlement, known as La Villa, was quite large and once housed about two hundred to four hundred people. The Hohokam in this vicinity lived in this area about AD 450 to AD 900. An earlier survey of the site was done in 2002 while digging the ground for the neighboring

Archaeologists found pottery, tools and pit houses during the Hohokam dig. *Author's collection.*

homeless shelter. La Villa was first discovered in the late 1920s and early 1930s and mapped out again in the 1980s.

The Hohokam were an agrarian people who turned the arid high desert of central and southern Arizona and northern Mexico into green farmlands and villages. They lived in the region for nearly 1,200 years, between AD 300 and AD 1450. The Hohokam culture collapsed around AD 1450. The people abandoned the area and mysteriously vanished. The name *Hohokam* comes from a word meaning "those who have gone" or "used up" in the language of the Pima Indian tribe—almost a ghostly reference to this vanishing tribe. Many of the Hohokam village sites show the remains of major irrigation canals, which supplied most of the settlements on the north side of the Salt River in Phoenix.

During the two weeks of November 2010, the archaeologists uncovered walls, doorways, steps, hearths, storage pits, holes for canopy poles and many pot shards. The team of workers was expecting to find about fourteen pit houses but were delighted when twenty-two former dwellings of the Hohokam were uncovered. Ironically, an ancient burial ground in the old settlement lies beneath the dead pioneers buried in the old Pioneer & Military Memorial Park (cemetery).

Sadly, the archaeological dig was re-covered with dirt once the study was complete, and the trencher tore away the floors of the ancient dwellings at a depth of twenty feet in order to complete the Phoenix storm drain project. But the ghosts and memories of the lives of the Hohokam will remain.

One morning, I was down at the cemetery doing a bit of volunteer work. I was out in the Porter Cemetery section, picking up garbage and papers that had blown into the grounds. Inside one of the fenced-in family plots I found a piece of Hohokam pottery painted yellow with an orange-red spiral center. I stopped what I was doing and took the shard into our offices to show the other volunteers. As they marveled over the artifact, I went back outside to finish my cleanup task. I walked back to the family plot and found that another plastic bag had landed inside the iron fencing. I leaned across the three-foot-high barrier to grab the bag. Suddenly, it was as though someone pushed me from behind, and I knew I was going to fall inside the burial plot! I tumbled forward, fearing I was about to be impaled by the pointed ends of the iron fence and then later embarrassed as the subject of an oddity story on the evening news. I envisioned the headline: "Cemetery Lady Impaled Herself on Iron Cemetery Fencing." Then, I was still. The whole cemetery was still. I looked down to see if there was blood. My blue jeans had been ripped,

Debe Branning sits among the relics of the Hohokam dig. *Author's collection*.

and there was a surface scratch on my thigh. I carefully stood back up. I knew what had happened. I had displeased the Hohokam spirits by removing the piece of pottery. I marched right back into our offices, grabbed the pottery shard and placed it under the soil in the family plot where I had discovered it. Lesson learned. Never remove a piece of Hohokam pottery from a site.

For more information on the Hohokam culture, visit the Pueblo Grande Museum & Archaeological Park at 4619 East Washington Street in Phoenix, Arizona.

"Sisto": The Old Gravedigger of the Phoenix Cemetery

Many Phoenix residents have family or friends buried in the old Loosely Cemetery, one of the seven cemeteries included in the Pioneer & Military Memorial Park (cemetery). It's always important to see the final resting place of the dead properly cared for and well kept. Therefore, you will enjoy the *grave matter* of this cemetery tale.

As members of the board of directors of the Pioneers' Cemetery Association in Phoenix, Arizona, myself and the volunteers of this mighty group dedicate our Thursday mornings and afternoons to tidying up the old cemetery, doing research on burials and "residents" and arranging tours and open-house events for guests who are curious about the interments of some of Phoenix's early pioneers.

In 2015, we organized a Grave Marker Preservation Committee led by PCA member Cindy Lee. The preservation team's mission statement is "to conserve and protect the historic physical remains, grave markers, artifacts, and buildings of Pioneer & Military Memorial Park and provide a safe, accessible community resource for present and future generations."

But they weren't the first caretakers of the cemetery. This historic cemetery has suffered from lack of care from time to time in the past. Even as far back as 1910, weeds, mesquite brush and other desert growths had overrun the cemetery until it looked more like a jungle than a plot of sacred ground.

Sisto Lizarrage (nicknamed "the old Mexican"), who for a quarter of a century served the Phoenix community as the official grave digger, finally decided to take some action in the matter. The 1910 conditions of the grounds were repulsive to this gentleman, who had dug many a burial plot in the city graveyard. Knowing personally a majority of those who had on one sad day or another joined in a mournful procession to the cemetery, he resolved to do something about the overgrown weeds at his own expense.

Sisto put a force of four men to work for a week, then reduced the team by one or two men and kept at the job for another week. By that time, he had put the cemetery in pretty good order. He not only cleaned off the weeds and brush but also straightened up fifty-two tombstones that had either fallen or were leaning in the soft ground, silent testimonies of the neglect of living friends.

Sisto invited the public, or at least those who had a personal interest in the care of the cemetery, to go and see the beautiful cemetery. He was rather proud of his work and had good reason to be—everything he did was voluntary, and he knew he would not get paid for his hard work.

We believe that Sisto is the guardian of the cemetery. Throughout history, it has been believed that a cemetery has an appointed guardian, a dearly departed soul who was left behind to protect the cemetery grounds and the deceased, not only from visiting humans but also from evil forces. This is one of the reasons why folks have reported hearing

Reenactor Chance Houston portrays Sisto Lizarrage during a cemetery history walk. *Author's collection.*

disembodied voices in cemeteries telling them to leave. It is believed the cemetery guardian is vigilantly making sure no one trespasses on the graves of those interred there—a guardian spirit who takes the phrase "rest in peace" quite literally.

There are times when the members of the Pioneers' Cemetery Association are alerted of water leaks, erosion or vandalism in the nick of time. They venture into the cemeteries armed with rakes, hoes and garbage bags to tidy up the old graveyard. Sometimes, they notice that trees have been trimmed or rocks carefully placed to mark a historic tombstone. Is this the work of the City of Phoenix landscapers, or is the spirit of Sisto Lizarrage diligently tidying up the cemetery he loved?

OLD BOOT HILL CEMETERY DUG UP IN DOWNTOWN PHOENIX

A few old caskets predating 1890 were discovered by construction crews laying the foundation of the new Maricopa County Sheriff's Office administration headquarters in Phoenix, Arizona, on May 14, 2012. Some caskets were empty, while others contained human remains and Native American artifacts. Skeletal remains of two small children were found, along with small fragments of adult bones scattered within the rubble.

The construction tract, located near Fifth Avenue and Madison Street, was the site of the first cemetery burial grounds in early Phoenix. These first burials occurred around the late 1860s to 1870s, when the graveyard was at the far southwest section of Phoenix, away from business and residential activity. It is not known how many burials were in the first cemetery, as records were incomplete, lost or destroyed. Some of Arizona's and Phoenix's important pioneers were once buried in the "boot hill" cemetery. King Woolsey, Johnny Le Barr, Luke Monihon and three-year-old Cassie Smith were among the early burials. A few of the original burials were the victims of the Old West, hanged or shot by lawmen or victims of disease and tragedy.

After Phoenix was incorporated as a city in February 1881, citizens and community leaders became concerned that the first glimpse of Phoenix had by travelers on the train was a dilapidated cemetery. In 1884, several fraternal organizations and the city government purchased Block 32, Neahr's Addition, keeping the eastern half to establish their own cemeteries and selling the west half to others for cemetery use. Many families and the city moved their loved ones from the original cemetery to the new one at Thirteenth Avenue and Madison Street. But, as often happens in reinterments, several of the graves were left unclaimed or missed altogether. The city reburied the unclaimed bodies in a common grave in what is now the Pioneer & Military Memorial Park (cemetery). Some of the burial records from both the new and old cemeteries are unfortunately lost. Restless spirits were left behind to wander the warehouse district and could be the source of the paranormal activity in the area.

The Fifth and Madison site was later given to the school district and has stayed in city or county government hands for many years. The vacant lot has become the site of the new county law enforcement redevelopment. Will the new Maricopa County Sheriff's Office be open to hauntings from the ghosts of the unclaimed bandits, robbers and thieves of Phoenix's past? Only time will tell.

Logan Simpson Design completed the archaeology, recovery and documentation of the remains, along with the guidance of the Arizona State Museum.

The members of the Pioneers' Cemetery Association rallied for the remains to be reburied in the historic City Cemetery located at the Pioneer Military & Memorial Park (cemetery). After all, this would have been the location of their 1884 reburial if their remains had been discovered over a century ago. The historians scanned the cemetery for a known vacant plot

A reburial for fourteen unknown Phoenix pioneers was held at the PMMP City Cemetery. *Author's collection.*

that could be used for the fourteen lost pioneers. Documentation showed that the vacant Greenhaw family plot was available, as the family had been reinterred at Greenwood Cemetery long ago. Its ornate gated fencing was still in place.

After all of the research and documentation were completed, it was unanimously agreed that the pioneers should be placed with their loved ones in the old City Cemetery. Greenwood Memory Lawn provided the labor and equipment for the burial. The Pioneers' Cemetery Association welcomed guests to the Pioneer & Military Memorial Park (cemetery) on Saturday, February 22, 2014, for a long-anticipated "Pioneer Reburial Dedication" of the remains of the fourteen early Phoenix pioneers.

With all said and done, everyone felt it was finally the proper time to celebrate the lives of these hardy pioneers. Reverend Philip Rye led folks dressed in western mourning attire out to the mass gravesite. A tombstone was donated with funds provided by Messinger Mortuary. After the blessing and prayer were recited, one by one, the period-dressed attendees tossed a white carnation onto the mound to honor the dead.

Dedication plaque for the reburial of several early Phoenix pioneers. *Author's collection.*

Gravesite photographs were captured—much like they did in the days of old to commemorate the event.

Special thanks to the PCA Reburial Committee and all its hard work to make this day happen.

Pioneer & Military Memorial Park
1313 West Jefferson Street
Phoenix, AZ 85007

HUNT'S TOMB

I remember visiting Papago Park, home to the Phoenix Zoo, and exploring some of the hiking trails. I noticed a large white pyramid towering high above a hill, overlooking the landscape and antelope habitat. The locals would tease and ask, "Do you know who's buried in Hunt's Tomb?" I would naively ask, "Who?" They would immediately laugh and point, "Hunt, of course!"

At first, I did not believe them. I had never heard of such a thing—a man buried overlooking a zoo? I became so obsessed with the story that I made my former boyfriend drive me up to the monument so I could see for myself. That was the afternoon I learned that Arizona's first governor, George E.P. Hunt (seven terms in office), was buried there. Also entombed are his beloved wife, in-laws, daughter and a son-in-law. It is still one of my favorite places to visit, and what a great view he selected as their final resting place.

George E.P. Hunt was born in Huntsville, Missouri, on November 1, 1859. His family moved west, and he spent many of his growing years in Globe, Arizona. He was sworn in as Arizona's first governor on February 14, 1912, followed by six additional terms, ending in 1932. A portly gentleman, he often referred to himself as the "Old Walrus." He was a supporter of reformed government and was either revered or feared by his followers. Hunt passed away on December 24, 1934, and was laid to rest beside his wife in the Hunt Mausoleum.

I was still curious to learn why Governor Hunt chose a pyramid as his burial monument. A pyramid represents the primitive mound from which Egyptians believed the planet Earth was created. The shape of the pyramid represents the descending rays of the sun. The upper chambers were intended as a magical device to attract the sun god Ra on his journey

Hunt's Tomb rises above the Phoenix Zoo in Papago Park. *Courtesy of Wikimedia.*

across the sky. The daily encounter with Ra would allow the dead to assume the role of the great sun god in the afterlife. Others say the pyramid was designed as a resurrection machine pointing to the stars in the heavens. He had a great plan in mind!

The archaeological discovery of King Tut's tomb in 1922 created a worldwide appeal for anything Egyptian. The Egypt Craze, or art deco, as it was nicknamed, was very popular in jewelry design, clothing fashion and building architecture. George Hunt and his family even traveled to Egypt in the 1930s to explore the great pyramids and monuments. These trips sparked his desire to locate the perfect spot to design and build his very own pyramid so he could be buried in a mausoleum for all eternity.

Hunt was granted permission from Congress to build his thirty-foot-by-twenty-foot pyramid on a small piece of the 2,050 acres that had been set aside as Papago Saguaro National Monument. The portion of land now belongs to the City of Phoenix and is in a secluded area of Papago Park. It has a concrete foundation and is covered with four-inch white polished tiles. The eerie pyramid can be seen from almost anywhere in the park. The tomb is the most visited Arizona governor gravesite.

As the mausoleum was being constructed, Governor Hunt was quoted as saying, "The people of this state have been good to me and in my last sleep I want to be buried so that I may in my spirit look over this splendid valley that in years to come will be a Mecca of those that love beautiful things and, in the state, where people rule."

The spirit of George E.P. Hunt has a great view of Phoenix and the haunted Arizona State Capitol today!

Hunt's Tomb
625 North Galvin Parkway
Phoenix, AZ 85008

5

PIONEER LIVING MUSEUM

The Pioneer Living History Museum is a thirty-minute drive from central Phoenix. On arrival, visitors are invited to explore more than ninety acres of land that comprise a nineteenth-century reconstructed town. The buildings are authentic and are historically reproduced.

Plans for the Pioneer Living History Museum took root in 1956, when a group of history-minded people formed the Pioneer Arizona Foundation. They had become concerned about the razing and demolition of historical buildings in the state Arizona as a result of new construction by land developers. The main goal of the foundation was to save some of the historical buildings that had been built between 1870 and 1910. The members of the foundation believed that by saving these buildings and by creating an atmosphere of the era, future generations would benefit by learning about the lifestyle of the early pioneers of the West. The museum had its grand opening in the winter of 1969. At this writing, there are thirty historic buildings to explore. The museum is open to public tours, school tours and special events. The living museum is considered a "Classroom Without Walls."

Of course, when they moved and preserved the historic buildings, some of them came with pioneer spirits of the past. Paranormal teams such as the MVD Ghostchasers, Arizona Desert Ghost Hunters and Phoenix Arizona Paranormal Society (PAPS) have experienced unexplained phenomena during their investigations.

Phoenix Living Museum entrance sign. *Courtesy of the Pioneer Living Museum.*

The Phoenix Arizona Paranormal Society was formed in 2004. One of its main objectives is to help owners of homes experiencing paranormal activity, but they also conduct tours and are involved with community events. Currently, there are about eight members in the group, including two cameramen. Jamie Veik came on board in 2012 and has risen to the title of lead investigator. PAPS has led paranormal investigative tours at the museum complex on and off for several years and carry the most data in their files. I spoke with Jamie, and he was gracious to relate some of their experiences throughout the historic buildings.

VICTORIAN HOUSE

The stately Victorian House was built in the early 1890s on an eighty-acre homestead in Phoenix owned by John Marian Sears. The homestead was graced with orchards of apples, peaches, pears and almonds. There was a pumphouse and windmill blowing in the desert breeze and even a dairy. Sears lived there with his wife, Mary, and three children. The house, originally located on North Seventh Street in Phoenix, was one of the earliest total wood-framed homes in the Phoenix area.

Volunteers and docents in the building have heard footsteps and felt the sensation of being watched.

PAPS investigator Veik noted:

> We once filmed an apparition moving from the main living room to the piano room. We also filmed a light moving in and out of the curtains as if it was trying to hide. A photograph of what appears to be a rod-shaped light anomaly was captured by the front porch. One of our team members had her pant leg pulled by an unseen force as an EMF detector spiked. A child's voice and woman's voice have both been recorded in the house as well as a man saying "I'm Tired." Countless EVPs have been captured in front of the house and on the front porch—the most impressive being a woman stating that "it's cold out here" even though it was actually the middle of summer. We also captured a man saying 'hi' as we walked up the front steps.

Flying V Cabin

The Flying V Cabin is another original structure from Young, Arizona, and was built around 1880. It was transported to the pioneer museum from Canyon Creek. The building has a unique feature. Notched gun ports were constructed in the walls for protection against Indian attacks. It was once raided on July 17, 1883, during the Battle of Big Dry Wash—the last Apache Valley war in that area. The Indians stole their horses but did not damage the house.

Information in the museum files indicate that the building was erected by John Tewksbury Sr., the patriarch of one of the families involved in the famous Pleasant Valley War between the Grahams and Tewksbury families.

Veik reported, "The most relevant capture was the word 'weapon' on SB7 Spirit Box during a tour."

The Flying V Cabin was especially constructed for protection against Indian attacks. *Courtesy of the Pioneer Living Museum.*

ASHURST CABIN

This cabin is the 1878 boyhood home of Henry Fountain Ashurst, Arizona's first senator. He gained national recognition as the "Silver-tongued Orator of Congress." Born in Nevada, the future senator came to Arizona at age four. He and his family resided a short time near Williams, Arizona.

The family lived about one mile east of Ashurst Lake in a box canyon. Prescott was one hundred miles and two mountain ranges away. There were no nearby neighbors. The family consisted of his sheep rancher father and his hardy pioneer mother, who gave birth to two of their children in the cabin. One sister died of pneumonia in the cabin. The family lived there until 1893.

The Ashurst cabin was moved piece by piece from the box canyon at Ashurst Springs to its new location at the Pioneer Museum in 1968, where restoration funding brought it to its current glory.

Jamie Veik recalled an event on one of the tours. "One of the SB7 Spirit Boxes captured a man saying 'you're grumpy,' a female entity stating 'a couple' after an investigator questioned 'how many spirits are here?' And, after being asked 'how are you?' in Spanish, a female voice said 'I don't speak.'"

MERRITT HOUSE

John and Emma Merritt sold their farm in Nevada, Missouri, and moved to Arizona in 1910. The Merritts and their two sons, Glenn and Melvin, bought a one-hundred-acre farm irrigated by the Arizona Canal, which had been completed in 1885. Their daughter Beryl was born on the farm in 1915, and it was her home until 2008, when she donated it to the Pioneer Living History Museum.

The three-room house had a large pantry that was later converted into a bathroom. The sleeping porch wrapped around three sides of the house, providing additional living space when needed. The kitchen, a separate outdoor structure called a "summer kitchen," kept excessive heat away from the main house in the hot Arizona summers. Another building brought from its previous location was the Water Tower. It was used to store water. The Merritt boys raised pigeons in its base. There is also a Granary and Carriage House from the Merritt properties.

"This was an interesting location," Veik nodded. "A bathroom door opened on its own—hitting a member of the paranormal team as he felt an energy field pass through him. Doors on the dresser opened on their own. We were unable to photograph anything in the main bedroom at times. There were also the sounds of heels walking in this same main bedroom. We recorded an EVP of a man saying 'teapot' as we entered the kitchen area."

NORTHERN HOME

Another simple, rustic building is the Northern Home, which was once nestled in Newman Canyon, about twenty-five miles southwest of Flagstaff. It was built sometime around 1885. It was once the home of Jeff D. Newman, who arrived in the Arizona Territory about 1886 with his wife, three sons and five daughters. The Marshall Lake Cattle Company donated the building to the Pioneer Living History Museum. This was a large 1880s cabin for the busy cattle-ranching family. The loft once extended the entire length of the building to accommodate the children's sleeping quarters.

"A tour guest was touched on the shoulder in the Northern Home," said Veik, "And we also received multiple SB7 Spirit Box responses including 'Get out,' and 'Don't talk like that.' After being asked if we were bothering the spirits inhabiting the home, a male stated his name was 'John.'"

OPERA HOUSE

James Howey was building a two-story structure and soon entered a contract with the Goldwaters to use his building as a general store. The Goldwaters opened their first store in Prescott using Howey Hall and kept their business there for three years.

Howey sold the building to Levi Basford, who constructed a stage on the second floor and opened a theater with a seating capacity of 200 to 250 people in 1882. The Opera House—still known as Howey Hall—featured famous celebrities of the time, such as John Drew and the beautiful Lillie Langtry. He remodeled the building, adding dressing rooms and installing upholstered chairs. There was even an ice-skating rink on the main floor.

The building was gutted in 1891, and the theater was moved to the ground floor. At the grand opening of the new theater, local thespians performed Gilbert and Sullivan's *H.M.S. Pinafore.* By 1894, the Opera House was declared unsafe and eventually closed.

It has served as a secondhand store and Prescott's fire station. In May 1959, Howey Hall was torn down. The bricks were numbered and acquired by Pioneer Arizona and used in an authentic reconstruction of the building as it stood during its Opera House period.

Melodramas staged in the Opera House serve to show the form of entertainment often found in early communities. The audiences were able to participate vocally by booing, cheering and shouting for the traveling cast of actors.

A Phoenix paranormal team, Arizona Desert Ghost Hunters, talked about their experience in the Opera House:

One of the team's favorite places to explore has been the Pioneer Arizona Living History Museum. In 2004 the team spent the night on six separate

Songstress Lillie Langtry performed in the reconstructed Opera House. *Courtesy of the Pioneer Living Museum.*

occasions, locked into the premises with only a caretaker present. During these outings various activities were recorded in both the Victorian house and the farmhouse. The favorite building however, is the opera house from Prescott. A team member placed a digital recorder on a chair in front of the stage at the opera house. We locked the door and proceeded to walk with the caretaker to the far side of the village to take pictures. Upon returning at 2:00 a.m. we began to review the recorder. What we heard was astonishing. For over forty minutes there was nothing but static on the recorder, then without warning the group began to hear sounds of a loud train depot. The screeching of steel on steel, loud banging like cars being coupled and uncoupled, muffled voices and many other loud noises. That lasted for exactly twenty-one minutes then there was only static noise again. Keep in mind the closest railroad tracks are almost twenty miles away.

The MVD Ghostchasers learned that an apparition was sighted in the upstairs area of the Opera House during a wedding reception. One of the groomsmen had dashed up the back staircase to grab a clothing bag he had placed over a chair in one of the dressing rooms. Without thinking, he quickly opened the door to the room. Embarrassed, he turned red and froze in his tracks. He thought he had walked in on one of the bridesmaids by mistake. But to his surprise, this lady dressed in period clothing did not even notice his presence and suddenly disappeared before his eyes.

The PAPS team had a few encounters in the Opera House, too. "We have picked up a voice multiple times asking for 'help'. A female entity has been documented several times on the stage, apparently performing, because EMF levels rose and fell with the interaction of applause and cheering. After being asked 'will you dance for us?' we captured a female stating 'no one will see.' We also captured a female sadly sighing, and someone telling us to 'sit down' as we walked into the building to investigate."

Blacksmith Shop

The Blacksmith Shop is a reconstruction of Middleton & Pascoe's barn that once stood in Globe, Arizona, based on a photo from the 1870s. It has double doors at the front and back of the building wide enough for a team and wagon to pass through. The floor is packed dirt, much like it would have been back in the day. Even though the building is not original, Jamie Veik says it's still thriving with paranormal activity.

"We have experienced multiple KII hits and other EMF activity, disembodied voices and metal clanging sounds. EVPs captured include a woman saying 'I'm Cold', 'Help' and a male humming a song."

Staff at the Pioneer Restaurant and Saloon believe it holds the energy of a visiting cowboy ghost. Perhaps he returns to have a drink served from the cherrywood bar built in 1861. While investigating the Saloon, the PAPS team captured an EVP of a gentleman stating he could not breathe and heard another gentleman's voice outside the Saloon door saying, "Oh Hell." They also heard the name *Rachel* over and over on a SB7 Ghost Box. PAPS team members have been followed by a gentleman that likes to touch you on the shoulders and whisper in your ear.

MVD Ghostchaser Gary Tone was a former Tempe, Arizona police officer. He often told the story of a strange event that happened while driving a prisoner to a detention facility north of Phoenix on Interstate 17. It was late at night and very dark along the freeway. He noticed a gentleman in period clothing and a top hat on the right side of the roadway carrying a satchel. Gary and his prisoner watched in disbelief as the man whisked across four lanes of freeway in the direction of the Pioneer Living Museum grounds.

The Pioneer Living Museum sits parallel to a former stagecoach route—perhaps still a drop-off destination for some of its former ghost riders. When the sun goes down, the spirits begin to roam the haunted locations of the property, making it a ghost town in so many ways!

Pioneer Living Museum
3907 West Pioneer Road
Phoenix, AZ 85086

6
MYSTERIES OF THE UNDERGROUND

BETH EL SYNAGOGUE

The Beth El Synagogue once stood on the northwest corner of McDowell Road and Third Avenue in the Encanto neighborhood of central Phoenix. The synagogue was headed by Rabbi Harr Z. Schechtman and opened on March 4, 1951, with 416 members. The building was the first new synagogue for the Beth El congregation.

In the early territorial days, Jews in Phoenix had to meet in one another's homes, local halls and gathering places for religious services and celebrations. Phoenix's first synagogue, Beth Israel, opened in 1921 at the northwest corner of Culver and Second Streets and met the needs of Orthodox, Conservative and Reform Jews.

A few internal conflicts flared, so the Beth El congregation, with a conservative Orthodox focus, was formed in 1930. Its first place of worship was the back of Goodman's store in downtown Phoenix. In 1932, they worshiped in what was a former Protestant church at Fourth Street and Fillmore.

The 1951 Beth El Synagogue on McDowell could easily hold 575 worshipers, and the basement hall could handle another 750 people. The congregation, composed mostly of Jews of European heritage, had a high percentage of Holocaust survivors.

Beth El Synagogue closed in 1965 and now houses a pawn shop. *Author's collection.*

The Beth El congregation grew so large that during High Holy Days they worshiped together at the Star Theatre—now known as the Celebrity Theatre. The synagogue building was sold in 1965, and the congregation moved to a new property at Glendale and Twelfth Avenues.

The old synagogue building on Third Avenue and McDowell Road was sold and revamped into a pawn shop. The shop's owner boasted of a discovery of four secret passageways in the basement near where the former social hall once blossomed.

Nobody knows for sure just where the hidden passageways went. It was not uncommon for synagogues to have secret passageways leading out of the building due to threats of anti-Semitism. The rabbis and congregants wanted extra escape routes should it become necessary to make a quick exit.

When asked, the pawn shop manager stated he had not seen much paranormal activity except for the night when he and two other employees heard three loud bangs downstairs in the basement. Startled, they quickly locked up and headed out of the door.

Beth El Synagogue (now Cash America Super Pawn Shop)
300 West McDowell Road
Phoenix, AZ 85003

THE GOLD SPOT BOWLING ALLEY

For more than a half century, the Gold Spot Bowling Alley, an abandoned underground bowling mecca, lay under Central Avenue and Pierce Street. It has been an often-discussed but rarely seen piece of Phoenix's history and lore. The Gold Spot opened in 1935 on the southeast corner of Central and Pierce, directly across from the Westward Ho Hotel. Between 1939 and 1950, the Gold Spot Bowling Alley occupied the basement area of the Nielson Radio and Sporting Goods Building.

Bowling became a popular pastime following World War II, with leagues popping up all around the Valley. "Split Happens!" The subterranean structure hosted bowlers and nighttime revelers until 1950, when it was closed and largely forgotten by almost all Phoenicians. The Nielson Building was demolished in 1991.

A few determined urban explorers searched the sidewalks and found remote access points via tunnels below the Westward Ho and missing panels of sidewalk glass that once provided light for the subterranean bowlers. Look closely and you can still see glass blocks on the otherwise abandoned lot, which allowed sunlight to filter through to the bowlers below. According to a 2003 story in the *Arizona Republic*, it's now "little more than a cellar held up by concrete columns," though the words "Please Stay Back of Foul Line" are painted on one of the support beams, while a painted bowling-pin mural enhances another. A few painted lane grooves remain on the floor.

Many of the vault lights in the sidewalk at the southeastern corner of Central and Pierce are still there. Vault lights became a part of the urban streetscape in the 1950s to provide natural lights to the basements of commercial buildings. They were safer and cheaper than using oil and gas lamps to light the basement areas. The basements of these buildings extended under the sidewalks, and the vault lights provided the businesses with more rentable space. In the evenings, the glass lenses would emit an eerie glow from the light of the businesses below.

Progress "spares" no one. In 2008, just before construction of the METRO Light Rail was completed, the last known access point to the bowling alley

Glass sidewalk tiles offer light over the former Gold Spot Bowling Alley. *Author's collection.*

was filled with concrete, forever burying the elusive Gold Spot Bowling Alley and all its secrets.

Remember, an urban explorer adventure under the streets is not worth striking out—risking life, limb or legal trouble to try to locate this secret location for yourself. But feel free to pass on the legend, now that you know it's actually true. Although the Gold Spot is long gone, the mystique of this unique, hidden Phoenix bowling alley still lives on.

The Gold Spot Bowling Alley (now caved in due to METRO Light Rail)
621 North Central Avenue
Phoenix, AZ 85004

PHOENIX'S BAT CAVE

There is a little-known place of terror and mystery in Phoenix. A hidden asphalt pathway leads to the notorious Phoenix Bat Cave, home to thousands of Mexican free-tailed bats that breed every summer near an isolated canal. Every evening at dusk, a massive number of bats takes flight, streaming out of the cave-like tunnel to feed on flies and mosquitoes during the night.

The Arizona Canal stretches nearly 39 miles from east of Scottsdale through Phoenix and into Peoria. It is just a part of the 132 miles of canals

Bat watch information. *Author's collection.*

operated by Salt River Project, a utility company, to bring water and power to Greater Phoenix. The 2-mile-long irrigation drain was built several decades ago to help with flood control. Management coordinators of the Arizona Game and Fish Department believe the hidden canal cave has the perfect temperature for the bats to live in and to breed and raise their young.

The modern canal system dates back more than one hundred years, when it was developed to serve Phoenix's agricultural needs. But the origins of the canals stretch into ancient history. Between AD 300 and AD 1450 the native Hohokam people lived and farmed in the Salt River Valley in what is today's metro Phoenix. They built some five hundred miles of ditches to bring water from the river to irrigate crops. In the late 1800s, more than four hundred years after the agricultural Hohokam mysteriously disappeared from central Arizona, Anglo settlers followed the vestiges of these irrigation ditches to shape the current canal system.

Bats have gained a spooky reputation through the years because of movies that feature rabid bats and vampires. Bats have always had a bad rap, but mostly, we like to be afraid of bats—just like we like to sit in fear and watch

Phoenix Bat Cave draws bat enthusiasts during warm-weather months. *Author's collection.*

a scary movie. Sometimes, our anxiety is reinforced near Halloween, when all of our childhood fears are placed in front of us. Ghosts, goblins, zombies, witches, vampires…and bats!

You can enjoy the live-action bat show each evening. Bats are harmless and won't get into your hair—that's merely a myth! They are fascinating and delightful little creatures with a reputation they do not deserve. I do not know how they became associated with Dracula, but perhaps it is because vampire bats live in Mexico and parts of the South. In the 120 years since Dracula came on the scene and spooked us into believing bats are bad, we're beginning to get a grasp on the truth. They are not nearly as dangerous as people think, although rabies can be an issue.

The Phoenix Bat Cave is about a two-minute walk along the canal path from Fortieth Street and Camelback Road. Look for signs that read "Bat Parking." The asphalt path is on the north side of the Arizona Canal. Follow the canal west about two hundred yards, past the office building and parking garage. You will know you are in the right spot when you begin to see city signs reading "Bat Watching Area," not to mention noticing the overwhelming odor of bat guano. The path takes you to the top of the tunnels.

On some evenings, it will take about ten minutes for the bats to fly out of the drain and into the night. Their goal is to hunt for food before returning to the cave in the morning to begin their daytime snooze. They generally stay in the area from May until October, when they migrate south of the border for the winter months.

Phoenix Bat Cave
5080 North Fortieth Street
Phoenix, AZ 85018

7

HAUNTED MANSIONS

EVANS HOUSE

The Evans House was built by Dr. John M. Evans in 1893 and is located near the Arizona State Capitol building. The house was used as a residence for him and his wife, Jennie, as well as his professional medical office. The two-story brick Queen Anne, Victorian home has an unusual onion-shaped dome over the front entrance, accenting the wraparound front porch. This unique dome roof earned the home the nickname "The Onion House" by early Phoenicians. The ground floor has seven rooms and was used as the family residence. It boasted eight-foot pocket doors that opened rooms into one large gathering space with fifteen-foot ceilings. The upper floor served as Dr. Evans's practicing office of medicine and had to be reached by a separate outside stairway.

Evans was a physician who dabbled in real estate and mining businesses on the side. Called a "Phoenix Capitalist," he often traveled, investing more properties into his growing empire. He resided in the home until 1904.

In 1908, the Oscar Mahoney family moved into the house. Oscar Livingston Mahoney (1839–1915) was a Confederate veteran and became the first superintendent of the Arizona Territorial Insane Asylum and served as a county coroner. His wife, Virginia (1848–1924), was one of only four women licensed to practice medicine in the Arizona Territory.

The domed-roof Evans home is nicknamed the "Onion House." *Courtesy of Wikimedia.*

The unique house was listed in the National Register of Historic Places on September 1, 1976.

Colleen Sulzer and I stopped in to visit the staff of the Evans House one morning after hearing that they have experienced some light paranormal activity. We were greeted by Joseph Roth, who was more than happy to share his unexplained tales.

"I've heard there were ghosts in the Evans House and been waiting to see one for myself," he chuckled. "I walked out of my office space to look for a file. A minute later I returned to see the maintenance guy standing in front of my desk, 'pale as a ghost.' I asked him what was wrong. He stood numb, pointing to my desk, trying to tell me he just saw a ghost standing there and watched it suddenly fade away. The man never returned back to our building to work again."

We walked around the ground floor of the unique office space and asked Joe if he ever heard mysterious sounds or noticed strange odors.

"Well," he thought for a moment. "Every once in a while, when I come in early to work, I have heard the click of one of the doors closing upstairs. When I go up there to secure the building, I find all the doors wide open."

Joseph stated that he has become used to the mysterious noises, and they don't alarm him anymore. A grin spread across his face as he pointed to the wall and a mysterious eight-inch dribble resembling a bloodstain about ten feet above the floor.

"We came into work one morning and found this!" He motioned to the eerie red line. "There were three more eight-inch lines about this same height in the boss's office, too! We had no idea what they were, or how they were placed way up there! She made the maintenance crew come in and paint over the marks in her office right away—but I thought it would be neat to leave *this* mark the way it is!"

The Evans House is not always accessible to the public and is currently used as the home for the Arizona State Historic Preservation Office, which is always in need of "spirited" volunteers.

The Evans House
1100 West Washington Street
Phoenix, AZ 85004

NORTON HOUSE

The grand Norton House was built in 1912 for college professor and veterinarian Dr. James C. Norton. He was the son of a successful Iowa cattle grower. Upon finishing first in his class of veterinary medicine at Iowa State University, he stayed at the college as an assistant professor until he made a decision to move west for his health and settled in Phoenix. Dr. Norton brought his wife, the former Clara Tufts, and family from Ames, Iowa, in 1892. Norton became the first territorial veterinarian of Arizona in 1893. His first veterinary office was located at 144 West Washington Street.

Norton was elected president of the United States Sanitary Livestock Association in 1904, was president of the Phoenix Chamber of Commerce in 1916 and president of the Arizona Farm Bureau. He was also involved in the YMCA and the Phoenix Rotary Club and was a member of the First Presbyterian Church for nearly sixty years.

One of the first things the doctor noticed on moving to Phoenix was that there was no Young Men's Christian Association (YMCA). He quickly rented a storeroom so meetings could be held, and Dr. Norton led the first YMCA building program fund drive, an organization that still strives today.

By 1912, Norton was ready to leave his veterinary practice and purchased two hundred acres of land just west of the central Phoenix area. He started a dairy farm and built his impressive two-story house. The Nortons raised

The 1912 Norton House was home to early veterinarian Dr. James C. Norton. *Author's collection.*

their four children—James, Oakley, Victor and Marietta—amid the two-hundred-acre Norton Dairy Farm.

Back in late 1915 though the early 1920s, a lavish green front lawn was the scene for family gatherings and perhaps a game of croquet. The backyard of the home featured fruit orchards filled with plum, peach and apricot trees.

The Mission Revival house was accented with fan windows of the Georgian era. Guests entered the home over a wide porch. Double doors were topped with the same Georgian look. The living room entry had a cozy fireplace of gray stone along the east wall. To the south was a library, and just north of the sliding pocket doors, the family retreated to a spacious dining room. The wainscoting, large built-in buffet and beams were showcased with beautiful mahogany woodwork. Over the buffet, light streamed through a leaded glass window highlighted with stained-glass sprays of grapes and vines. A walk-through pantry and china closet separated the dining room from the kitchen. Nearby was a maid's quarters, a bath and rear screen porches.

The upper floors boasted five bedrooms, one of which had its own fireplace. A large bathroom off the center hall served the family and guests. There were two screened sleeping porches that ran the length of the back of the house to aid in those Phoenix hot summer nights.

Before Dr. Norton sold his property, the house boasted one of the country's earliest evaporative swamp coolers. This was a large bin covered with cork and fiberglass, which was kept wet. Electric fans inside drew the dampened air through a basement window into the home.

In 1930, Dr. Norton began selling portions of his property to the City of Phoenix for the new Encanto Park and golf course. The city finally took over the property in the spring of 1935. The insurance policy was not in effect if the house was found empty. Duty-minded employees took turns spending the night in the huge mansion. In the early days, the recreation department used only three of the rooms. Business was conducted from the living room and dining room while caretakers occupied the rooms upstairs.

The Norton House remains the offices of the Phoenix Parks and Recreation Department today. Colleen Sulzer and I parked on the south side of the mansion near the old carriage house and walked up the steps to the front door. We were greeted by the office staff, who seemed eager to talk about the history and a bit of the mystery of the stately home.

The Norton carriage house remains as part of the Norton property. *Author's collection.*

"The ladies who worked as our previous staff were here a long time, and they were the ones that had the most interesting stories and experiences," the girl at the front desk told us. "They did mention that the sound of footsteps could frequently be heard up on the second floor and that they often heard children laughing and playing."

She also recalled hearing a story concerning one of the maintenance crew members. "It seems the groundskeeper glanced over at the house, and through a window he saw a woman dressed in a white Edwardian-era floor-length gown slowly walking across the floor *inside* the house."

"Wearing all white in the spring and summer was very popular at that time—especially with the warm Phoenix weather," I noted.

"I bet that groundskeeper was pretty nervous about coming into the house after that!" Colleen giggled.

Just before we were ready to leave, the girl at the desk remembered her own unexplained encounter with the spirited Norton family.

"I used to sit over there—at the desk on the other side of the room," she pointed. "There were a few times when I would feel like 'someone' just might be in the room and all of a sudden I could smell cigar smoke. Now, I don't know whether Dr. Norton smoked a cigar or not—but I do know these days smoking is not allowed in or around the building, so wherever that cigar aroma was coming from remains a mystery to me!"

So, the next time you are at Encanto Park for that family birthday party or company picnic, keep in mind that *Encanto* is the Spanish word for "enchanted"—a fitting name for Phoenix's charming 222-acre park. Be sure to look across Fifteenth Avenue and thank the Norton family for their hindsight regarding the needs of the growing city of Phoenix. And be sure and keep an eye out for the enchanting "lady in white."

The Norton House
2700 North Fifteenth Avenue
Phoenix, AZ 85007

ELLIS–SHACKELFORD HOUSE

This historic home was designed by local architect R.A. Gray and built in 1917 for prominent physician William C. Ellis. The Ellis-Shackelford House is important for its architectural design, materials and early technological achievements, such as automatic flush toilets, push-button light switches, central vacuum system and an underground rainwater cistern.

The home was constructed with elements of the Prairie style, common in midwestern states. It also has the detailing work of the Craftsman style, which was popular in early Phoenix. The house features three stories and a basement. It has hardwood floors and hand-painted, globe-style chandeliers. Hand-pressed red bricks from Colorado comprise the exterior walls, known as "wire-cut" because of their rough appearance. The mahogany wood trim and banister, staircase and built-in bookcases were constructed from imported mahogany trees from the Philippines and milled on the property.

During the period from the mid-1910s through the 1930s, this section of Central Avenue was nicknamed "Millionaires' Row" for the beautiful mansions of similar style that lined the road. Because the Ellis-Shackelford Home is the only unaltered survivor of these early North Central Avenue mansions, it was placed in the National Register of Historic Places in 1983.

Dr. Ellis was a native of Ohio and moved to Phoenix in 1907. He helped organize the Arizona Deaconess Hospital (now Banner Good Samaritan), serving as the chief of its medical staff. The home was the mainstay of

The 1917 Ellis-Shackelford House is the last remaining mansion along Millionaires' Row. *Author's collection.*

three family generations. Dr. Ellis's daughter and her husband, J. Gordon Shackelford, lived in the house until 1964. It then became a boys' home and later headquarters for the Arizona Historical Society offices and museum. The building is now owned by the City of Phoenix and home to the Arizona Humanities.

The good news is the family still has ties to the home. Missy Shackelford, the great-granddaughter-in-law of Dr. Ellis, works as an administrative assistant for Arizona Humanities. When the *Arizona Republic* interviewed Missy about ghosts remaining in the house, she stated, "It feels peaceful and friendly—almost like a protection."

That sense of protection was felt one evening after an event. She closed the shades and walked over to the box to set the building alarm. She checked the alarm box and discovered it was reading "fault." It was indicating to re-check the northwest sunroom, which was her office—and Uncle Jim Shackelford's old bedroom. She went back upstairs but did not find anything that could possibly trigger the motion detectors.

"I checked all the windows and thought 'this is ridiculous' because everything is latched shut," she shrugged her shoulders. Was the spirit of Uncle Jim playing a silly prank or just keeping her on her toes?

Marshall Shore, Colleen Sulzer and I popped into the Ellis-Shackelford House one afternoon for a private impromptu tour of the historic home. Once again, Missy was happy to give the grand tour, which included escorting us down to the basement of the home where children once played in order to stay cool during the hot summer months. The basement had also been used as a workshop, storage area and quarters for servants and grounds maintenance workers. She also let us climb up to the upstairs attic floor—low clearance for some visitors, but not for Colleen and me! This was the area used for parties, ballroom dances and even dorms for a short-lived boys' school.

Missy told us that her boss, Brenda Thomson, had an unexplained experience where she heard footsteps on the stairs and then silence. Another employee, Dyadria Fajardo, had her own encounter at the Ellis-Shackelford House when conducting a tour of the attic with her boyfriend. She gave him a quick look around the house and headed to the door that opens to the staircase to the attic. The couple closed the door behind them and went up the stairs to take a peek at the old ballroom dance floor. As they glanced around the area, the two explorers stopped in their tracks! That door at the bottom of the staircase was now wide open—suggesting to the two investigators that they better get out of there!

Even though her coworkers are a little shaken up every now and then, Missy Shackelford doesn't mind the uninvited ghostly guests. She's convinced they are her deceased family members coming back to visit.

"My father-in-law and his brother Jim had a lot of fun in life. They loved to laugh and loved to play, and I have a feeling they enjoy having people in this home," Shackelford said. "In fact, at one time there was a miniature train on the grounds complete with tracks that encircled the house! Just imagine how popular that was with the neighborhood children!"

She added, "It's very comforting to me. I have a different frame of mind because I actually knew these 'spirits.' Now, my coworkers might not feel as comfy as I do. If the 'spirits' are opening doors, I think they're just reminding us that we need to be open and inviting, and we need to bring the community in."

Cindy Lee and I arrived at the Ellis-Shackelford House for a Halloween seasonal event of storytelling by our friend Marshall Shore. We parked the car across the street and strolled over to the front yard seating, grabbing a cookie from the refreshment table along the way. I noticed Cindy staring up at the window of the back bedroom.

"Who was that man watching us from that upstairs back window?" Cindy asked Marshall after his presentation.

"Funny you should ask," Marshall chuckled. "In just recent months, 'Uncle Jim' Shackleford passed away and that room was his bedroom. The staff believes he is still coming around the house to check on things."

Shore also related a story of a gentleman staffer who was constantly the subject of office pranks. On many a morning he would walk into his office only to find his desk in disarray or papers and pens rearranged in a strange manner. "Grandma 'Shack' loved to play pranks on the boys," Missy giggled. "Perhaps it was her way of letting the male office worker know he was 'one of her boys now!'"

The Ellis-Shackleford House
1242 North Central Avenue
Phoenix, AZ 85004

Rosson House

Looking somewhat like a glamorous version of the "Munsters" mansion from the old television show, the Rosson House was built between 1894 and 1895 and sits on its original foundation in busy downtown Phoenix. Named for Dr. Roland Lee Rosson and his wife, Flora Murray Rosson, the Victorian mansion changed hands numerous times before being purchased by the City of Phoenix and restored to its original condition. It now serves as a historic house museum located in Phoenix's prestigious Heritage Square.

The house is built in the Stick-Eastlake Queen Anne style of Victorian architecture. It was designed by a prominent San Francisco architect, A.P. Petit. Sadly, Petit died in the same month of its completion. The architecture displays numerous features contributed from several different cultures, such as an Asian moon gate, Italianate hooded windows and a French octagonal turret.

The house boasts of many original features, such as parquet wood floors, nine Gib doors, a Queen Anne–style grand staircase and even the kitchen sink! The cost of the house in 1885 was $7,500, a fair amount of money for the day.

In 1879, Dr. Roland Rosson arrived in Phoenix, where he promptly established himself as a general physician and surgeon. The doctor practiced medicine on and off in Phoenix from 1879 until 1897. Besides his career as a physician, Rosson also had an interest in politics. In 1882, he was listed on the Democratic primary ticket, and in 1884, Rosson was elected Maricopa County coroner and public administrator. He served two terms as the county treasurer (1890 and 1892). On May 7, 1895, Rosson was elected to the office of mayor of Phoenix. His position as mayor was short-lived. After many disagreements with the city council, he resigned from office on April 6, 1896. He remained active in the political scene in Phoenix.

Dr. Rosson married Flora B. Murray in Phoenix on August 11, 1880. The Rossons had a total of seven children; Irene, Vivien, Floy, Norma and Clyde lived to adulthood. Two of the children died in infancy. Their first son, Roland Lloyd, died at age five weeks and is buried in the Pioneer & Military Memorial Park (cemetery). An unnamed daughter died in birth.

The Rosson House was built with every modern convenience of the time, such as electric lights, hot and cold running water, an indoor upstairs bathroom and a telephone. Other Victorian mansions on Monroe Street were similarly equipped. The Phoenix streetcar line ran down Monroe before turning north on Seventh Street, so the Rosson family and other Monroe Street residents had only to walk out their front doors to board it.

The Rosson House was built in 1895 and is the last of the grand mansions on Monroe Street. *Author's collection.*

The Rossons continued to own the home and the remainder of Block 14. However, during the winters of 1895–96 and 1896–97, the Rosson family rented their home to Whitelaw Reid, an influential Republican and head of the *New York Tribune* newspaper. No sources indicate where the Rosson family resided during that time. Reid had a lung condition, and his doctors recommended he travel to Arizona for his health.

In June 1897, the Rossons sold their lovely home and the north half of Block 14. The family moved to Los Angeles, California, by July 27, 1897. The exact reasons for their move are unknown. Newspaper accounts suggest that the Rossons may have had financial difficulties. According to delinquent tax records listed in the newspapers in 1896 and 1897, both Roland and Flora owed back taxes. Renting their newly constructed house to Whitelaw Reid also suggests that the Rossons needed additional income. The family may also have moved for other reasons. Roland Rosson's obituary in 1898 read, "he removed with his family to Los Angeles on account of the educational advantages."

Not much is known about the brief time Dr. Rosson spent in Los Angeles. After a long illness of several weeks, he died on May 12, 1898. At first, rumors began to surface that his death was considered suspicious and possibly a suicide. It was known that shortly before his death Rosson purchased life insurance policies from several different companies. But alas, an autopsy and a coroner's jury in Los Angeles ruled the death to be a result of gastroenteritis. Little is known about the fate of Flora's life as well. She passed away in Los Angeles from "tubercular laryngitis" at age fifty-two on September 9, 1911. Her death certificate listed her occupation as "household duties," aka, housewife.

Other families thrived in the Rosson house through the years. Aaron and Carrie Goldberg purchased the house on June 3, 1897, from the Rossons for $10,000. The Goldbergs were a prominent Jewish couple in Phoenix. Aaron co-owned the fashionable Goldberg's clothing store. He too was involved in politics and civic activities. As a member of the nineteenth and twentieth territorial legislatures, Goldberg wrote the bill that permanently located the state capitol in Phoenix. The Goldberg children included Hazel, Selma and Chester (Chet), who, according to his obituary, was born in the Rosson House.

On September 7, 1904, the Goldbergs sold the house and property to S.W. Higley. Steven W. Higley lived in the Rosson House with wife Jessie Freemont Howe, sons Thomas and James and daughter Jessie Jean. The Higley children kept a pet fawn on the front lawn of the property and would occasionally sneak the animal into the house, it scampering up the staircase to the top floor. Grandma Higley would eventually realize she had a hooved visitor upstairs and scold the mischievous children. Laughter and giggles filled the home as the children and fawn dashed back down the staircase and out the front door.

The Higleys sold the Rosson House and portions of the larger lot to the Gammel family on August 22, 1914. The Gammels owned and lived in the Rosson House longer than any other family. Earlier, William Gammel had been a gambler in Jerome, Arizona. In 1904, he married Frances Christopher, a Hispanic woman from Tucson. The couple had three daughters: Annie, Wilma and Atlanta Georgia. Gammel was a co-owner of the Capitol Saloon on East Washington Street. Shortly after he purchased the Rosson House, Prohibition became law in Arizona and put a financial burden on Gammel's business. The Gammels covered their hard times by renting out furnished rooms in the spacious Rosson House.

The Gammel family continued to live in the Rosson House until 1948, operating it as a boardinghouse. They made several changes to the once grand home, including walling in porches, subdividing floors and adding multiple kitchens and bathrooms. After 1948, the Rosson House changed hands multiple times but continued to operate as a rooming house, eventually becoming somewhat of a "flop house" and showing signs of disrepair.

The City of Phoenix purchased the Rosson House and the remainder of Block 14 in 1974. The Rosson House was restored through a community effort involving the City of Phoenix, dozens of local institutions and hundreds of volunteers. It now operates as a house museum that interprets the history of Phoenix through several revolving programs and displays. Tours of the house offer visitors an opportunity to explore the lifestyles of Phoenix families of the early 1900s.

Rosson House docents have reported a spirit who constantly locks doors, and they have heard an unknown entity wandering throughout the building in the late hours of the night. The volunteers have also witnessed phantom heat coming from an unlit fireplace.

A guest on one of Marshall Shore's "Haunted Phoenix" tours told the group she was doing some interior design work at the Rosson House, when suddenly the ladies began to notice the distinct aroma of fresh roses. "It was not the season for the roses to be blooming outdoors," she smiled. "And there were no fresh floral arrangements inside the house."

Some docents tell stories of a ghost that lingers in the home, alarming hearts with unexpected footsteps descending down the staircase. Is it the spirit of one of the former ladies of the house rushing down the staircase to greet her guests? Or could it be the ghosts of those playful Higley children, still trying to conceal their unconventional house pet?

Both visitors and employees claim to have seen ghosts lurking outdoors on the property grounds of the Victorian mansion as well. Rumors speculate that it might be the ghost of a former caretaker who was shot and killed on the grounds in the area of the carriage house in the 1980s and still tending to his work at the grand mansion on Monroe Street.

The Rosson House
113 North Sixth Street
Phoenix, AZ 85004

HELEN ANDERSON HOUSE

The Helen Anderson House is a well-preserved "fairytale" English Cottage Revival structure in midtown Phoenix. Characteristic of the style, the distinctive roof is composed of green wooden shingles and rolled eaves that simulate a thatched roof. The English Cottage Revival design was very popular after World War I. The Cotswold cottage architecture of the Helen Anderson House is a unique style of home originally from England—commonly known as "storybook" style. One can almost imagine Hansel and Gretel knocking on the storybook home of the wicked witch in the forest. Cotswold homes are known for their pseudo-thatched roofs, arched doorways, steeped arched gables and brick or stone siding. A tall chimney with a battered top is prominent from the street side.

It was built in 1920 as a residence for Helen Anderson, the wife of insurance company organizer Carl H. Anderson, and it is currently occupied by Hob Nobs Food & Spirits. This house replaced an earlier gabled-roof bungalow built about 1914. A 1922 *Arizona Republic* article

The Helen Anderson House resembles a whimsical storybook home. *Author's collection.*

described Mrs. Anderson's recently completed house as "charming to the eye and mind with a vision of old England." Later widowed, Helen Anderson continued to live in the house until about 1924. The house was subsequently purchased by Colonel Dale Bumstead, a rancher, who lived there until the mid-1940s. The building was added to the National Register of Historic Places on November 30, 1983. The historic home is part of the historic Roosevelt Neighborhood.

Helen Fairchild was the daughter of Flagstaff sheriff John Fletcher Fairchild. He claimed his nose was broken in an early fight with Wyatt Earp in Dodge City, Kansas. Fairchild was also on the posse during the Pleasant Valley range wars. His old injury began to cause him great pain. He traveled to California, where surgeons operated on his nose. He came back to Arizona but did not feel much better. The pain eventually made him insane, and he was brought down to the Arizona Asylum in Phoenix, where he died three months later.

Helen married Carl Anderson in January 1914 in California. The young Anderson couple moved to Arizona and were soon the toasts of the town, often attending social gatherings and hosting parties. Carl was prominent in the Phoenix club circles and was a member of the Kiwanis Club, the chamber of commerce and the Phoenix Country Club. Helen entertained at women's club luncheons and organized gala parties. She was photographed driving her black Hudson Super-Six Sedan, proving it to be the "ideal warm weather car" to drive on the Arizona roads—perhaps a means of advertising for her husband's insurance business.

Carl H. Anderson died shortly after midnight at the Anderson residence on February 13, 1921. Death resulted from complications following an illness extending over a period of two years. He was only thirty-seven years old. His wife, Helen, and their son, Donald, were left alone in the house.

Helen eventually moved on with her life and sold her storybook cottage. The next couple to dwell in the home were Eva and Dale Bumstead— or the Colonel, as he liked to be known. Once he retired from military service, he took on another quest. Bumstead became widely known in California and Arizona as a horticulturist. He was the first to realize the commercial possibilities of the Cardinal grape, a large cardinal-colored table fruit. On his farm near Phoenix, Colonel Bumstead raised acres of Khalasa dates. His farm, Tal-Wi-Wi, was known as "the most valuable acre of farm land in the world." Eva was known as a society leader, world traveler and big-game hunter. Trophies brought back from their expeditions after hunts were displayed in the Museum of Natural

History in San Diego, California. Eva died in 1937; the Colonel stayed in the Phoenix area until he passed away in 1952.

More recently, folks in Phoenix will remember that, in the 1980s, the Helen Anderson House was the home of Jutenhoops, a novelty store that featured quirky gifts, cards and collectibles. Jutenhoops moved away in the 1990s, and the Helen Anderson House became a hip coffeehouse and art boutique named the Willow House. The Hodge family bought and converted the building to Hob Nobs Food & Spirits.

Immediately, rumors began to circulate about ghostly activity at the quant eating establishment. When the Hodges were ready to open for business, they found themselves mysteriously deadbolt-locked in from the inside and could not get out. After a few adjustments, things seemed to get back to normal until the front door suddenly blew open. They took it in stride, with the attitude that ghosts were welcoming them and a good omen for the new café. Owner Cherylin Hodge told us of a customer who snapped a photo of her child, only to notice a shadowy face of a different boy on the top half of the picture.

Megan Taylor and her friend Cassie—both intuitive—stopped at Hob Nobs for lunch one Saturday. Afterward, they walked to the rear of the building, when Cassie suddenly stopped in her tracks. "There's a spirit of a young Hispanic-looking man standing by the old unattached garage near the alley." They both stopped and watched as the ghostly gentleman stared at them and faded away.

Several weeks later, Cindy Lee and I stopped in the establishment to arrange a paranormal investigation of the building in the upcoming months. On our way out, I mentioned the experience my other friends had shared. I suggested we stand near the back wall of the alley. We shook our heads, as we were not picking up on any spirit energy at all. "How about walking down the alley a little bit?" I suggested to Cindy. She walked down and stood in the alley about midway alongside of the old garage. "I do feel a little bit of activity here. Can't say what it is—but if there is something back here, it is near this garage, not the back wall."

We may never know what the spirit lurking in the alley may be. A neighbor? A transient workman? Carl C. Anderson waiting to take one of his many vehicles for a spin? Perhaps something will drive us to find the answer.

The Helen Anderson House, aka Hob Nobs Food & Spirits
149 West McDowell Road
Phoenix, AZ 85003

SMURTHWAITE HOUSE

The historic Smurthwaite House graces the grounds of the Pioneer & Military Memorial Park (cemetery). The two-story brick home was designed by James M. Creighton and built in 1897 for $2,875. Coincidently, Creighton's twelve-year-old son is buried in the nearby Mason Cemetery. Smurthwaite House is an outstanding example of Queen Anne Shingle Style architecture. In addition to the Rosson House, it is one of the few remaining nineteenth-century buildings still standing in Phoenix.

Originally, the house was intended to be used as a boardinghouse. It was sold in 1903 to Captain Trustrim Connell, a Civil War veteran, and his wife, Anne, as a private residence. Their daughter Caroline Connell married Charles Frederick Smurthwaite at the residence in December 1907, and the couple later moved back into the home with her elderly parents. Granddaughter Carolann Smurthwaite was born in the house in 1918.

Ann Eliza Maffet Connell died in the home and was buried in Los Angeles, California. Trustrim and Ann Connell were married for fifty-three years. Captain Trustrim Connell passed away in the upstairs bedroom in 1937 at the age of ninety-three. He was buried at the side of his wife in California.

In 1931, Trustrim Connell deeded the house to Caroline, who became a collector and dealer in Native American art. In fact, Caroline opened the first gift and antiques shop at the Arizona Biltmore Hotel in 1929. The house was also used as a gift shop in the early 1930s.

Sadly, the Smurthwaite marriage ended in divorce in April 1934. Caroline and daughter Carolann continued to live in the house and cared for the ailing Captain Connell until he passed away from heart failure.

Caroline and Carolann Smurthwaite continued to be very involved in the Phoenix Art Community, active in the local DAR organizations, and their business thrived with the antiques and gift shop enterprise. Caroline passed away in the house in October 1971 at the age of eighty-nine.

Daughter Carolann continued to work with the collections of Native American art, doing business under her mother's name out of the Biltmore shop and using the parlor of the Smurthwaite House as a gift shop. Carolann never married and never moved away from her childhood home. She died within its walls in 1982 at the age of sixty-four. In her will, Carolann requested that the home be preserved and made available to the public.

The Smurthwaite House was donated jointly to the Phoenix Art Museum, the Museum of Northern Arizona and the Heard Museum. The three museums later offered it to the City of Phoenix. The city currently maintains the house and the Pioneer & Military Memorial Park adjacent to it.

In 1991, the Heritage Fund approved a grant of $50,000 to restore the Smurthwaite House to its glory years. Due to freeway construction and city plans for the neighborhood, it was decided the Smurthwaite House could not stay in the Churchill Addition, so it was relocated. The house made the news in 1994 as the three-thousand-square-foot dwelling made a landmark journey of twenty-six city blocks through the streets of Phoenix from its original site at 602 North Seventh Street to its current location at 1317 West Jefferson Street. Restoration work began in May 1998 and was completed in June 2001. On May 17, 2001, the Smurthwaite House was added to the National Register of Historic Places.

The first floor of the house is furnished in late Victorian style, thanks to generous contributions by donors. The Smurthwaite House serves as an archival library for information regarding historic cemeteries throughout Arizona and also as the headquarters for the nonprofit Pioneers' Cemetery Association Inc.

The 1897 Smurthwaite House was moved to its present location in the middle of a cemetery in 1994. *Courtesy of Wikimedia.*

The members of the Pioneers' Cemetery Association noticed a few odd happenings when the group began meeting regularly on Thursday mornings. Sometimes, the ladies who were first to arrive would feel the presence of a man and smell the aroma of cigar smoke in the gift shop area. They reported hearing footsteps on the second floor, distant chatter or items found out of place. Nobody thought much of it—after all, it was an old house and it sat in the middle of a historic cemetery.

I received an interesting e-mail one afternoon from a former city employee who once kept offices in the Smurthwaite House when it was located on Seventh Street.

"Is the house still haunted?" began her inquiry.

That was all that was needed to grab my attention. She went on to say that the City of Phoenix group did office work in the room now showcased as the dining room of the house. She recalled an incident that startled her on a summer afternoon. She had just finished organizing some paperwork and found herself the last remaining employee in the building—so she thought.

"As I was finishing my filing and addressing a few envelopes I suddenly heard someone pacing back and forth on the second floor. I called up to see if another employee was still up there working on a project but received no answer. I decided my work was done for the day and locked up. I never worked alone at the Smurthwaite House again!"

The former city employee had my full attention. She went on to say there was a full-time maintenance/security man who lived on the property of the Smurthwaite House during this period of time. At the end of each day, he turned down the lights and went upstairs to one of the large bedrooms to sleep. He slumbered very meagerly, on a cot, and was always ready to begin his work early each morning. One evening, he climbed into his sleeping bag after a particularly hard day. He was just about ready to drift off to sleep when he began to hear someone walking from room to room on the second floor. He thought it was an intruder and grabbed the baseball bat he kept near his cot. The footsteps stopped, and suddenly there was a loud crash from the bedroom closet as though something large and heavy slammed to the floor. He covered his head with a wool blanket and tried to sleep. The next day, he checked the top floor, including the closet, and found everything in place. As expected, he did not last very long on the job.

The mischievous pranks and noises did not let up after the house was moved to the Jefferson Street location. The new house and cemetery groundskeeper, Tammy, had her own story to tell.

"I had gone upstairs to make sure all the window shades were closed before it was time for me to leave for the day," she recalled. "I was standing at the top of the staircase when someone—or something—nudged me on the arm. I thought someone was up there trying to get my attention, and I turned quickly to look behind me—only to find myself alone. This sure kept me on my toes, though. It taught me to never overlook even the smallest detail when closing up the house in the afternoons."

Cindy Lee and I brainstormed and came up with a plan to increase PCA's annual membership. We decided to gather a group of paranormal investigators and do a top-to-bottom ghost investigation in the Smurthwaite House. It would include cleaning up litter in the cemetery, a potluck dinner and a "lights out" investigation of the historic home. A one-year membership was included in the package. About eighteen ghost-hunting enthusiasts decided to take the challenge.

One of the highlights of the evening was when a male energy was spotted standing at the top of the staircase on the second floor. Cindy had led a small group of investigators up the stairs to note the EMF base readings, looking for areas with high magnetic field ranges. As they approached the last few steps, they looked up to see a man watching them as if he was there to welcome the inquisitive guests. This shadowy figure was spotted a second time much later in the evening. This time, he was standing in the hallway near the upstairs bathroom as the group prepared to conduct an EVP session.

Marge West was a longtime member of the Pioneers' Cemetery Association. She was the go-to gal when you needed to locate a grave marker in the cemetery or a historic biography of one of the dearly departed. As a founding member of the PCA, she was well respected by her peers. Marge's goal was to have a full-scale preservation team come in and save the remaining grave markers in the historic cemetery. Sadly, she passed away in the summer of 2013 before her dream became a reality. She is greatly missed by everyone at the Smurthwaite House, and we are grateful for all the information she documented through the years.

But is Marge really gone? Some of the PCA board members believe she is still hard at work and watches over the ongoing fulfillment of her dream of preservation at the cemeteries. Shortly after Marge passed over, Cindy came down the stairs to see the tiny gray-haired lady standing inside the entryway of the Smurthwaite parlor. She looked up and smiled.

"She was wearing her blue jeans and her favorite blue plaid blouse," Cindy noted. "It was later that evening we learned she had passed away."

Denise, one of the volunteers at the cemetery, carried bundles of Memorial Day decorations and flowers upstairs to a storage closet. It had been a long day, and she was anxious to head home and put her feet up. As she headed toward the stairs, she saw someone dart into a locked closet of an adjacent room. She dashed over to the closet and jiggled the locked door. She shrugged and tried to explain what happened to the other members of the group waiting to lock up downstairs.

Light footsteps are often heard pacing across the second floor during the board meetings. If the meeting agenda becomes a bit confrontational, a latch on a lower cabinet door clicks and swings open near the spot where Marge frequently sat during the meetings. Marge West, as well as the Smurthwaite and Connell families before her, lovingly remain in the house to preserve its history and their legacy.

Smurthwaite House
1317 West Jefferson Street
Phoenix, AZ 85007

8

FAIRY TALE CASTLES

MYSTERY CASTLE

The enchanting Mystery Castle is located in the foothills of South Mountain Park near the most southern tip of Phoenix. It was built throughout the 1930s by Boyce Luther Gulley for his beloved daughter, Mary Lou Gulley.

As a child, Mary Lou loved to hear fairytale stories of beautiful castles. The family would visit ocean beaches, where Boyce would create decorative sandcastles. She cried when the castles in the sand were washed away by the tide. Her father promised that one day he would build her a castle that would stand forever.

After learning he had tuberculosis in 1927, Gulley vanished from his home in Seattle, Washington, and settled in the isolated desert hills near South Mountain in Phoenix. He bought a large parcel of land and began to build a fairytale castle home from inexpensive scrap materials he gathered from various construction sites in the growing neighborhoods of Phoenix.

Gulley lovingly toiled for over fifteen years on a dream castle built especially for Mary Lou. Boyce Gulley died in 1945, having fulfilled the childhood promise he had made to his daughter.

Mary Lou and her mother, Frances Gulley, were notified that Boyce had passed away and that they somehow inherited a castle in the far-off desert land of the Southwest. They packed up their belongings and headed to the

Secrets abound at the Mystery Castle near South Mountain. *Author's collection.*

booming town of Phoenix. To Mary Lou's relief, there were no waves to wash away this castle.

Their story made headlines around the world. A *Life* magazine story (January 26, 1948) called "Life Visits a Mystery Castle: A Young Girl Rules Over the Strange Secrets of a Fairy Tale Dream House in the Arizona Desert" made Mary Lou and her mother local celebrities. The magazine dubbed it the "Mystery Castle," because the writers were not sure what they were going to find when they came out to the desert oasis to do the story. A *Life* photograph featured Mary Lou posing atop the cantilever staircase leading to the roof of the house. That same year, the two enterprising Gulley women began offering tours of their home for fifty cents per guest.

The first few years living in the castle were hard on Mary Lou and her mother. They resided several miles from downtown Phoenix and needed to find a way to earn some money to pay the bills. Their Mystery Castle Tours became very popular with the new tourist boom of Phoenix, and they have continued for over sixty years.

People from all around the area came to see the sprawling eighteen-room home filled with paintings and Southwest antiques. The castle, made of

Portrait of Mary Lou Gulley, the lady of the castle. *Author's collection.*

adobe, pieces of steel, glass and auto parts, boasted thirteen fireplaces, a chapel, a cantina and even a dungeon. The room that divided the chapel and cantina was nicknamed "purgatory." A pump organ that showcases the grotto is said to have been the property of a lady named Elsie, nicknamed the "Widow of Tombstone." It is said she buried six husbands in the old Boot Hill Cemetery.

The castle is an architectural wonder in the Valley of the Sun. It was built with scrap material and odd objects that Boyce Gulley hauled home each evening when the development of Phoenix was at a rapid growth. Outside, you will find beautiful glass and stonework in the gardens.

It also has several spirits residing within its walls. Mary Lou observed the spirit of her father standing on a stairway. Famed psychic Jean Dixon confirmed his presence.

The MVD Ghostchasers conducted a Paranormal Workshop investigation tour of the Mystery Castle in 2002. It was a great honor to have Mary Lou Gulley present on the expedition that late afternoon. When Mary Lou finished the tour, she sat outside on the patio and told us of her wonderful experiences in the unique castle. She assured us that sometimes it was a hard life, but she wouldn't have wanted to change it in any way. Then we asked her about the ghosts and spirits.

"I have seen my father's spirit in the castle many times," she smiled. "He is still protecting myself and the Castle."

Then she remembered another story. Late one night, some out-of-town friends decided to pay her a surprise visit at the castle. Mary Lou made sure the gates were locked and secure before sundown. Her friends drove to the locked gate and parked the car. As they approached the entry gates, they claim they were driven away by a pair of Doberman watchdogs.

"The funny part was my faithful pair of Dobermans had passed away years before." Mary Lou chuckled. "I believe their animal spirits are still patrolling the grounds."

As we toured the unique home, a few of us passed by the staircase that led to a private upstairs sleeping quarter. Trisha Dolan, a medium and psychic, pointed to the staircase and asked someone to quickly snap a photo with their camera. She witnessed a vision of a man standing on the steps and didn't want the workshop crew to miss this rare Kodak moment. Could it have been the spirit of Boyce Gulley?

Mary Lou passed away in 2010 at the age of eighty. The property is now maintained by the Mystery Castle Foundation, a nonprofit organization. The castle is on the Arizona Registry of Historic Places. Visitors can sign up

Paranormal investigators explore the Mystery Castle grounds. *Author's collection.*

online for daytime tours or join in on an occasional nighttime paranormal investigation with Amy Currie Schrader, owner of Haunted Scottsdale Ghost Tours.

The final line on Mary Lou's obituary read, "The Castle remains open to the public so that all may explore the wonders that lie behind its magical doors."

The Mystery Castle
800 East Mineral Road
Phoenix, AZ 85042

TOVREA CASTLE

The unique architectural structure called Tovrea Castle was the vision of Italian immigrant Alessio Carraro. Carraro traveled to Phoenix in 1928 with a vision of building a fine resort hotel surrounded by a beautiful cactus

Tovrea Castle is often nicknamed the "Wedding Cake House." *Author's collection.*

garden. The plans were for the majestic castle to become the focal centerpiece of a subdivision of luxury homes. Although Carraro's big dream of a hotel/resort never came to be, he did build his fairytale castle.

Construction on Tovrea Castle began in the spring of 1928 on forty-three acres of undeveloped desert land known as Warner Heights. The property was located along the Tempe Road, just four miles east of Phoenix. Carraro removed most of the vegetation from the native granite terrain, except for the many saguaro cacti.

The final touches of Tovrea Castle were completed in January 1931. The devastating Great Depression put a damper on Carraro's plans of developing the land for monetary gain. To add to the troubles, he realized that the livestock pens built on neighboring lots would also halt his big expectations. He put the property up for sale and continued his work on the castle. In 1931, Carraro sold the completed castle and its surrounding forty-three acres to cattleman and butcher shop owner Edward A. Tovrea.

Tovrea Castle is a pine wood and stucco building erected in a three-tier design, giving it a strong resemblance to a traditional wedding cake—hence the local nickname the "Wedding Cake House." It has historically eclectic and European architectural influences, including parapets surrounding the roofline of each tier. The castle is lit up each night with seasonal colored light bulbs along the roofs and fences.

In 1919, E.A. Tovrea moved from Bisbee, Arizona, with his second wife, Della, to the sparsely populated Phoenix area about a quarter mile west of the Warner property to build the Arizona Packing Company along Tempe Road. Edward soon became a local cattle baron whose nearby stockyards reportedly accommodated more than 300,000 cattle annually and was one of the largest feedlots in the United States.

E.A. Tovrea died of pneumonia in 1932, and Della remarried in 1936 to William P. Stuart, publisher of the *Prescott Courier*. The couple lived in the Prescott area during the summers and in the castle during winter months. Stuart died of natural causes in 1960. Both of Della Tovrea's husbands died at the castle, adding to its mystery over the years.

Della Tovrea moved back to the castle and continued to make it her residence until 1968, when a devastating robbery occurred. Della was getting up in age. She lived alone and chose to make her living quarters on the main floor. She slept on a cot in the kitchen. One stormy November night, she was awakened by the sound of someone breaking into the castle from the upper floors. Della was a tough woman and carried a pistol with her to frighten people off the property from time to time. She fired the pistol through the

Old locomotive warning bell on the grounds of Tovrea Castle. *Author's collection.*

ceiling in the kitchen to try to scare the intruders away, but to her dismay, the robbers did not fear her warning shot.

The intruders tied the eighty-year-old woman to a chair and managed to escape with roughly $50,000 in cash, silver and jewels. Della managed to loosen the ties and tried to summon the caretakers, who lived elsewhere on the property, by call button and telephone. The lines had evidently been cut. Still in her nightgown, she braved the storm to ring the old locomotive warning bell outside the front door. They still did not respond. She was forced to walk to their nearby quarters to look for help. The weather and stress of the robbery were too much for the elderly woman. Della caught pneumonia and was confined to a nursing home, where she died a short time later, in January 1969.

Eventually, the castle fell into disrepair. In 1993, Phoenix voters approved $5 million to purchase and restore Tovrea Castle. A $4.5 million bond

Debe Branning and Cindy Lee attend a full-moon tour of Tovrea Castle. *Author's collection.*

authorized in 2001 helped the city expand its holdings around the castle to forty-four acres.

A friend, Mary Duer, participated on a guided tour of Tovrea Castle with her club, the Arizona Prospectors Association. The gentleman who was in charge of the activities for the club's event was a City of Phoenix employee and led the special Tovrea Castle tours at the time. The club members were invited to use their metal detectors to locate garden plant markers that were buried in the soil as an entertaining group activity. A member of their club, Leo, was the son or grandson of the Carraro family who originally built the mansion, so it was a special treat for him to be back at the castle.

Many guests on the tour asked the knowledgeable docent about "spirits," and he said, "officially, I will say no!" But he did have a story to tell them. He noted that a few of the restoration workers once told him about hearing a child playing ball on one of the upper levels. He didn't think much of it at the time until one day when he was using the bathroom on the upper floor. It was a quiet time of the day—after all of the workmen had left and gone home. He heard giggling and a ball bouncing toward the bathroom door. Of course, when he came out of the facilities, there was nobody there! In another incident, workmen found a child's bare footprint walking through the sawdust when there were definitely no children on the construction site.

Knowing the history of the families who lived there through the years, he could never pinpoint who the playful ghost might have been. The woman who lived there the longest, Della Tovrea Stuart, had several nieces and nephews who came to visit, but no children of her own.

Tours are offered during daytime hours. An occasional Twilight Super Moon tour provides a more intimate ambiance. Just a note: you can still see the bullet hole in the kitchen ceiling from the night of the robbery. Be sure to ring the old bell to perhaps awaken the spirits!

Tovrea Castle
5025 East Van Buren Street
Phoenix, AZ 85008

9
HAUNTED BYWAYS

JoJo's Alley

Nobody really knows how the story of haunted JoJo's Alley began. Most likely, it is just an urban legend, but the draw to visitors to the Phoenix suburban alleyway lives on. An alleyway is often described as a "narrow, pedestrian lane found in city areas which usually run between or behind homes and buildings. Some alleys were built to allow for deliveries such as coal or ice to the rear of the houses, or a place to set out one's trash or debris. Some alleys were paved while others were unmaintained dirt pathways" (*The Free Dictionary*, Farlax).

An alley can be a very intimidating place to be—especially after dark. Most alleyways are pitch black or dimly lit. Trash cans may line the pathway, with scattered discards and odors. In some cases, rats and other creatures searching for food roam around, hiding in corners. The homeless can be found searching for food or other treasures that have been tossed aside.

Many innocent people have met their demise in an alley and have returned to seek revenge for their death. Out of all of the so-called haunted alleyways in Arizona, there is none more widely known than Phoenix's JoJo's Alley.

To get to JoJo's Alley, one must travel north on Seventh Street. After you pass Glendale Avenue, stay in the right-hand lane and look for a sign that reads "E Circle Street." This is the location of the notorious

The entrance to the ominous JoJo's Alley. *Author's collection.*

JoJo's Alley, or "Dog Boy Alley," as it is also known. Turn right and drive slowly. New speed bumps deter a fast getaway in case you are chased by something unknown.

The ominous JoJo's Alley is a small, narrow street with asphalt paving. It is lined with mature oleander trees that are shaped over the alley—almost like a tunnel. It is a quiet passageway during the day, but when night falls, all the mysteries begin. Because of the lack of lighting and the creepy overhanging oleanders, the drive can be a frightening adventure.

Some of the ghostly claims are of strange lights chasing your vehicle. Urban legend boasts that mysterious lights appear out of nowhere and flash at anyone brave enough to drive down the dimly lit alley. Some drivers swear they have seen ghostly figures in the alley as their vehicle coasts slowly past the oleanders.

Other visitors to JoJo's Alley declare they have heard the sound of pounding fists hitting the roof of the vehicle as they made their fateful drive. That is enough of a reason to keep the windows rolled up!

There are still many mysteries surrounding this spooky alleyway. Where did the name come from? Just who was JoJo? Oh, and one more thing. JoJo's

Alley is a dead end (no pun intended). If you are brave enough to make it down the dark passageway, don't forget that you will have to turn around and drive back out the same way you came in—if you dare!

MALINDA'S ALLEY

For the longest time I heard the name "Melinda's Alley" on every walking ghost tour operating in Phoenix. The guide pointed to an alley area south of Monroe Street and east/west of Central Avenue. To my dismay, nobody seemed to know who Melinda (aka Malinda) was or why the alleyway bore her name.

Then one day I found a newspaper clipping about the death of Charles D. Poston (1825–1902), an aged pioneer and a grand piece of Arizona history known as the "Father of Arizona." The newspaper story mentioned that on June 25, 1902, Poston had been seen walking through Melinda's Alley, taking a shortcut to his adobe home not far off the alleyway. Poston died that evening on his property from an old illness. He fell "suddenly to the bare and dusty earth—there and then—without a struggle." Shortly after three o'clock in the afternoon, a Phoenix policeman made his rounds through Malinda's Alley. As he neared the old adobe structure occupied by Poston, he glanced to a narrow side passage that led to the rear of the building and noted seeing the body of a man stretched out on the ground. He immediately recognized the man to be Charles D. Poston, now broke and living out his last moments in a dilapidated adobe. His heart had finally failed him. He was almost laid to rest in the pauper cemetery, but someone came forth with funds so he could be buried in Porter Cemetery at the old Pioneer & Military Memorial Park. His body was moved to its final rest inside a pyramid tomb at the top of Primrose Hill near Florence, Arizona, in 1925. Now I had a lead and searched for copies of old Phoenix street maps. To my amazement, Melinda's Alley was listed on the city territorial maps.

The alley ran east and west between Adams and Monroe according to the original Phoenix plots, making it more of a dirty, rundown street. There were many small shacks and houses running along Melinda's Alley between First Street and First Avenue—a bit of a skid row with drunkards, gamblers and prostitutes. Camelback Mountain could be viewed far off in the distance, and the tallest building one could see was the old Adams Hotel—now the

Take a stroll down the dark and eerie Malinda's Alley. *Author's collection.*

site of the Renaissance Hotel. These days, it is still a dark, creepy alley that takes partygoers to a few hidden speakeasy bars and clubs.

But just who was Melinda? Was she a real person or an urban legend? The first step was to pull the 1910 and 1900 Phoenix pages of the U.S. Census documents. Bingo! Scanning the 1910 census, we found forty-five-year-old Manda Curtis listed as a widowed washwoman. The 1900 census reported her as thirty-six-year-old Malinda Curtis and running a boardinghouse. Digging deeper into the 1880 census, one can find Malinda Curtis working as a servant in Rapides, Louisiana. She offered Louisiana or Missouri as her place of birth on various documents. She was married, widowed and said to be a mother of one child.

We found Melinda Curtis in Tucson, Arizona, living as a courtesan on Maiden Lane in October 1890. The newspaper reported that Annie Miner and Melinda Curtis, alias Goldy and Roxie, came before Judge Mayer on a charge of assaulting a soldier from nearby Fort Lowell. The gallant soldier stated that he meandered into Maiden Lane by mistake and became involved in conversation with the ladies of complexion. They proposed the beer but he did not see it that way, whereupon he alleged that the ladies proceeded to beat his face and head. This being a bit too much for his martial blood, a warrant was issued for "Goldy and Roxie." Annie Miner (Goldy) spent one week in the Tucson jail. This might have prompted Malinda to move north to Phoenix.

The exact date of Malinda's coming to Phoenix is lost in the mists of the distant past, but it is estimated the year to be about 1890. More often than not, she had fallen into the hands of the police, but as a rule her misdeeds were trivial and a consequence of strong drink, for which she formed a great fondness.

Marshall Shore loves to tell guests on his Haunted Phoenix Bus Tour the tale of Malinda and "a pail of noodles." One autumn day in 1909, Malinda Curtis and John Morris were summoned to appear in Police Judge Thomas's courtroom in Phoenix. The judge, used to the alley squabbles, asked the pair what the argument was all about. Morris explained that he had been walking home, carrying a pail of noodles. He acknowledged that Malinda came along and insisted on having some of the noodles. He told her to help herself, and Malinda quickly grabbed two spoons. He brought a chair out of his house and sat down. An angry Malinda demanded to know why he didn't bring out two chairs so she could sit down, too! As John Morris held on to the ill-fated pail of noodles, she slapped him hard. This sent the noodles flying into the air, landing on top of her head. Malinda slapped Morris some more—he pushed her to the ground, with all those sticky noodles adhering into her hair. He started to laugh. The judge was not amused. Malinda's turn came. She accused John Morris of owing her five dollars. She told the judge she went to his house to collect the debt. Morris admitted he owed Malinda two dollars and promised to pay her soon. The judge fined them each seven dollars and sent them on their way.

Her mind was that of a child in a great many ways. Malinda seemed to have little comprehension of the meaning of "evil." In the opinion of those who came to know her best, her good deeds outweighed her sins. There was never a time when she was not willing to cook for or nurse the unfortunate sick, with never a thought of collecting payment.

As time passed, Malinda's form began to take on an unnatural roundness. She was afflicted with dropsy; that disease was partially responsible for her demise. The more immediate cause of her death, however, was the ravages of liquor. During the last few weeks of her life, Malinda saw "strange beasts in the air." At times, she seemed to have a genuine case of delirium tremens.

On October 28, 1910, Malinda Curtis died at her squalid little home

Malinda Curtis mural created by Hugo Medina and Darrin Armijo-Wardle. *Author's collection.*

in the alley in back of the Ensign Stable, just off North First Street. The passing of "Malindy," as she was familiarly known, was met by sorrow by a great number of people, both whites and African Americans. While she did not always walk the straight and narrow path, she was one of the warmest-hearted old women who ever lived and was always doing something for someone whose circumstances were even more destitute than her own. White folk as well as members of her own race were the recipients of her tender nurturing.

These friends came together to make sure she had a proper interment in Evergreen Cemetery. Be sure to look upward to the buildings that tower over Malinda's Alley just east of Central Avenue. Believe it or not, you will be rewarded with a sign that Malinda is still there, protecting those who walk the dark alleyway at night.

Malinda's Alley
Runs between Monroe and Adams Streets, and First Street and First Avenue
Phoenix, AZ 85004

PARANORMAL RESOURCES—TEAMS AND TOURS

Arizona Desert Ghost Hunters. www.adghosthunters.com.
AZ Paranormal. info@AZParanormal.com.
Crossing Over Paranormal. www.thecopscrew.com.
Friends of the Other Side. www.friendsoftheotherside.com.
Haunted Phoenix Tours. marshallshore@gmail.com.
Haunted Scottsdale Ghost Tours. www.hauntedscottsdaleghosttours.com.
MVD Ghostchasers. www.mvdghostchasers.com.
Phoenix Arizona Paranormal Society. www.phoenix-arizona-paranormal-society.com.
Phoenix Ghost Tours. https://phxtours.com/ghos t-tour.

BIBLIOGRAPHY

American Legion Post 1. "History of Post 1." www.post1az.org/post-1/ history.

Arizona Republic. "Good Deeds Outweigh the Sins of Malinda." October 29, 1910.

———. "Phoenix Hotel Held Up, Bandits Escape." September 24, 1941.

———. "Phoenix Treasure Hunt Is a Bust." October 15, 1975.

———. "Runs Amuck in Swanky Hotel." May 10, 1947.

———. "Tom Cat Adopts Theater and Is Now Its Mascot." January 5, 1929.

Arizona Republican. "A Ghost Story." August 26, 1893.

Arizona State Capitol. www.azlibrary.gov/azcm.

Atlas Obscura. "Phoenix Bat Cave." May 2017.

AZcentral.com. "Former Phoenix Synagogue Turned Pawn Shop with Secrets." March 2018.

———. "The History of the YMCA in Downtown Phoenix." February 10, 2015.

AZFamily.com. "Maricopa County: Unearthed Caskets Found in Phoenix." May 14, 2012.

Branning, Debe. *The Graveyard Shift.* Phoenix, AZ: American Traveler Press, 2012.

Combe, Ray. "Still Mighty at Ninety." Friends of the Orpheum Theatre. January 5, 2019. www.fototphx.org.

Copper Era and Morenci Leader. "Murder and Suicide in the Capital at Phoenix." May 7, 1912.

Ellis-Shackelford House. www.azhumanities.org/about-ah/ellis-shackelford-house.

George Washington Carver Museum. www.gwcmccaz.wordpress.com.

Mystery Castle. www.mymysterycastle.com.

North Phoenix Blog. "The Gold Spot: Phoenix's Underground Bowling Alley." May 25, 2015.

———. "Memories at Phoenix Union Station." June 3, 2013.

Pela, Robert L. "Majestic Ruins: Phoenix's First Baptist Church and More." *Phoenix New Times,* May 3, 2012.

Phoenix Historic Preservation Office. "The J.C. Norton House." www.phoenix.gov.

Phoenix New Times. "Arvizu's El Fresnal Grocery Store, Niki D'Andrea." December 8, 2010.

Phoenix Theatre. "History of Phoenix Theatre." www.phoenixtheatre.com.

Pioneer Living History Museum. www.pioneeraz.org.

Pueblo Grande Ruins. www.phoenix.gov/parks/arts-culture-history/pueblo-grande/about-the-museum.

Robins, Si. "J.M. Evans House." *Downtown Phoenix Journal,* December 1, 2010.

Rosson House. www.heritagesquarephx.org/visit/the-rosson-house.

Smurthwaite House. www.azhistcemeteries.org.

St. Mary's Basilica. www.saintmarysbasilica.org.

Sweet Old Buildings. "Winnie Ruth Judd." www.sweetoldbuildings.wordpress.com.

Tovrea Castle. www.tovreacastletours.com.

Village People. "YMCA" (song). Written by Victor Willis, Jacques Moranli and Henri Belolo.

Webb, Dewey. "Tip of the ICEHOUSE." *Phoenix New Times,* November 4, 1999.

"The Westward Ho Monthly Messenger." Victor Pawlak, editor for 2011–12 editions.

ABOUT THE AUTHOR

Debe Branning has been the director of the MVD Ghostchasers, a Mesa/ Bisbee, Arizona–based paranormal team, since 1994. The team conducts investigations of haunted, historical locations throughout Arizona and has offered paranormal workshops/ investigations since 2002. Debe has been a guest lecturer at several Arizona universities and community colleges. She has been a speaker at science fiction and paranormal conferences as well as historical societies and libraries talking about historic/haunted Arizona.

She has appeared in an episode of "Streets of Fear" for FearNet.com that aired in 2009, on an episode of the Travel Channel's *Ghost Stories* about haunted Jerome, Arizona, in 2010 and on Travel Channel's *Ghost Adventures*, "Old Gila County Jail and Courthouse," in 2018. She has traveled, toured and investigated haunted locations in the United States, England, Scotland, Ireland and Mexico.

Debe is the author of *Sleeping with Ghosts: A Ghost Hunter's Guide to AZ's Haunted Hotels and Inns* (2004), *Grand Canyon Ghost Stories* (2012), *The Graveyard Shift: Arizona's Historic and Haunted Cemeteries* (2012), *Dining with the Dead: Arizona's Historic and Haunted Restaurants and Cafes* (2017) and a series of three children's books, *The Adventures of Chickolet Pigolet: 1. The Bribe of Frankenbeans, 2. Murmur on the Oink Express* and *3. You Ought to be in Pig-tures*.

As a paranormal travel journalist, Debe traveled to Europe to cover haunted castles, jails, ships, inns, cemeteries and ghost walking tours. She has been the guest of several U.S. tourism departments, including Carlsbad, Historic Hotels of the Rockies, Salem and Biloxi.

Debe is a preservation activist with a special interest in preserving historic cemeteries. She is on the board of directors of the Pioneers' Cemetery Association and the Arizona Genealogical Advisory Board. She is also one of the cohosts of the Association for Gravestones Studies in Arizona.

Visit us at
www.historypress.com